Direction
Nacho Alegre
Omar Sosa

Associate Editor
Marco Velardi

Editor-at-Large
Albert Folch

Art Direction & Graphic Design
Albert Folch Studio

American Editor-at-Large
Michael Bullock

Food Editor
Leen Hilde Haesen

Administration
Víctor Abellán

Production Assistant
Eduardo Iborra

Distribution Consultant
Alexis Zavialoff
MOTTO

Translation
Paul Geddis
Débora Antscherl
Jonathan Bennett

Proofreader
Belinda Wicksteed

Printing
CA Grafica (Spain)

Cover image
Marco Velardi, London, 2008

Publisher
Apartamento Magazine S.L.

D.L.: VG 379-2008
ISSN 2013-0198

Distribution
Apartamento is distributed internationally by EXPORT-PRESS
T +33 (0) 01 40 291 451
F +33 (0) 01 42 720 743
dir@exportpress.com

with the exception of:

Spain by ATHENEUM
T +34 936 544 061
F +34 936 401 343
atheneum@atheneum.com

France by IMPORT-PRESS
T +33 01 40 291 451
F +33 01 42 720 743
dir@exportpress.com

Japan by UTRECHT
T +81 (0)3 5856 5800
F +81 (0)3 5773 6685
info@utrecht.jp

Switzerland by MOTTO
T +41 (0)764203557
www.mottodistribution.wordpress.com

If you would like to know more about distributing Apartamento in your store or can't find it in your country please write to:
info@apartamentomagazine.com

Head Office Spain
Llull 57, 7-3
08005 Barcelona, Spain
T/F +34 93 485 65 36
info@apartamentomagazine.com

Head Office Italy
Via Salutati 17
20144 Milan, Italy
contact: Marco Velardi
T/F + 39 02 36 56 82 20
marco@apartamentomagazine.com

Advertising
For advertising opportunities please write to:
ad@apartamentomagazine.com

Contributors
Adrià Julià
Anna Clerici
Antonio Montouto
Anri Sala
Arquitectura-G
Betta Marzio
Carlotta Manaigo
Catherine Krudy
Ekhi Lopetegui
Elsa Fischer
Enrique Giner de los Rios
FAR
Felix Friedmann
Giorgiana Ravizza
Jem Goulding
Joan Morey
Juan Moralejo
Karley Sciortino
Katherine Clary
Kiko Buxo
Klas Ernflo
Leen Hilde Haesen
Mathias Sterner
Markus Miessen
Max lamb
Mylinh Trieu Nguyen
Paula Yacomuzzi
RJ Shaughnessy
Silvia Orlandi
Wai Lin Tse
Ye Rin Mok

Thanks
Cyril Duval, Joerg Koch, Jamie Gray, Sean Beolchini, Hiroshi Eguchi, Linlee Allen, Massimo Torrigiani, Carolina Montpart, Isa Merino, Miquel Polidano, Kenneth Perdigón, Martino Gamper, Gemma Holt, Chris Moorby, Chiara Zappalà, Marc Serra, Amets Iriondo, Andrea Caruso, Adriana Rodriguez, Fernando Amat, Bruno Sosa, Ramón Ubeda, Ana López, Jon Sueda, Gala Fernández, Zak Kyes.

Many thanks to all contributors and advertisers.

A PARADISAL LIFE

BY KATHERINE CLARY

On Telegraph Hill we would spend hours over the eccentricities of their home. Childlike, I would eagerly climb the spiral metal staircase that brought me to the second floor. What spectacle waited for me evoked such curiosity that I often find myself, years later, referencing that familiar feeling of awe.

We all have those particular locations or objects that we store away in order to protect them. In an attempt to somehow preserve their sacredness, certain memories are oftentimes not spoken about at all, but instead catalogued away, protected from too frequent sentiment or nostalgia. Their San Francisco home was a safe haven of the mind, a spot in which I could retreat to, mentally or physically, and continually find solace in.

While my uncle boasted an impressive vintage metal toy collection, displayed beside the staircase like a stoic little army, it was their library whose image remains in my head, pure and untouched. It wasn't necessarily the content, though I learned to appreciate their vast collection as I grew older, but the timelessness and permanence of this wall that I found so intriguing. Scanning this library allows one to become a witness to the many photos and notes, spanning decades, which were slipped in between books of Henry James and Aubrey Beardsley, small relics of the past. They sat as reminders that this monument was older, much older than I, and held many things I was unfamiliar with, evoking a naïve and sometimes daunting wonder.

Stacked to the ceiling of the aging, wooden library were hundreds upon hundreds of books, from guides to the West Indies to manifestos from the 1920s and everything in between. And behind us, off the deck and just beyond a vast sea of green - the San Francisco bay. Bougainvillea, blackberry bushes and plum trees lay before the sea, which oftentimes for hours only emitted the faint horn of a tugboat. How idyllic! I sit now in a sweltering, concrete city, where no parrots perch on the balcony in search of plums, no freshly ground nutmeg sits in the marble mortar and pestle, and the morning sounds are not muted by the fog, but piercingly clear. Yet I know it waits for me, charmingly patient and serene, as it tends to be.

BREATHING SPACE

BY JEM GOULDING
PHOTOGRAPHY BY RJ SHAUGHNESSY

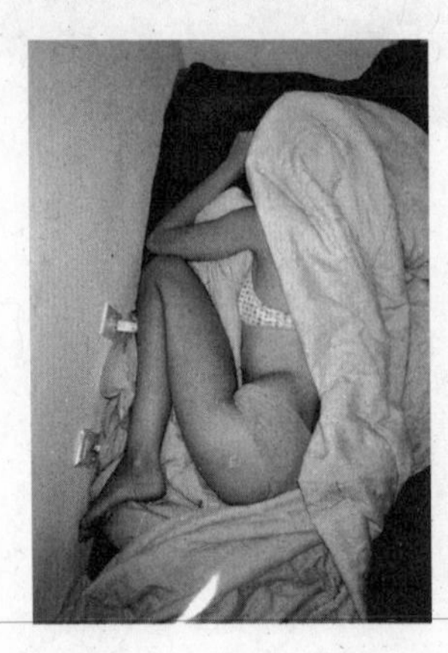

Apparently there is need of a routine here.
Some stability.
It's called order you say, and that's what
I'm lacking.

This room reflects a state of mind.
Bedlam.
Like me you say.
A beautiful mess.

I traced my flights on your globe yesterday.
Felt empty when my finger glided around
places I didn't get to.
Now I'm home.
Yet I feel homesick.

I've been away too long again, apparently.
Explaining myself is like a homecoming ritual.
Questions with no right answers.

It must be difficult to accept that you and
I want different things.
I wish it didn't eat you up.

I'm a gypsy if you say so.
Qualified by the fact I don't own a watch.
Or a credit card.
Freedom from obligation always.
But you're mistaken.
I know it won't last.

I hope you have some use for me stuck in
your box.
What if I decide to stick around this time?
Think about it.
What you will do without my disappearances?

I didn't want to fly back.
Home has a settled sound to it that scares the
shit out of me.
It doesn't mean I don't think about stuff.
I do.

When I'm away, I should write to you more.
You can read about the world.
Read about my world from the safety of your
world and feel involved.
Included.
Even though you are not.

I know you care.
But if you'd let me be, believe me when I say
it's not forever.
You'd love me for it.
Give it up.
You're going to hurt your feelings.

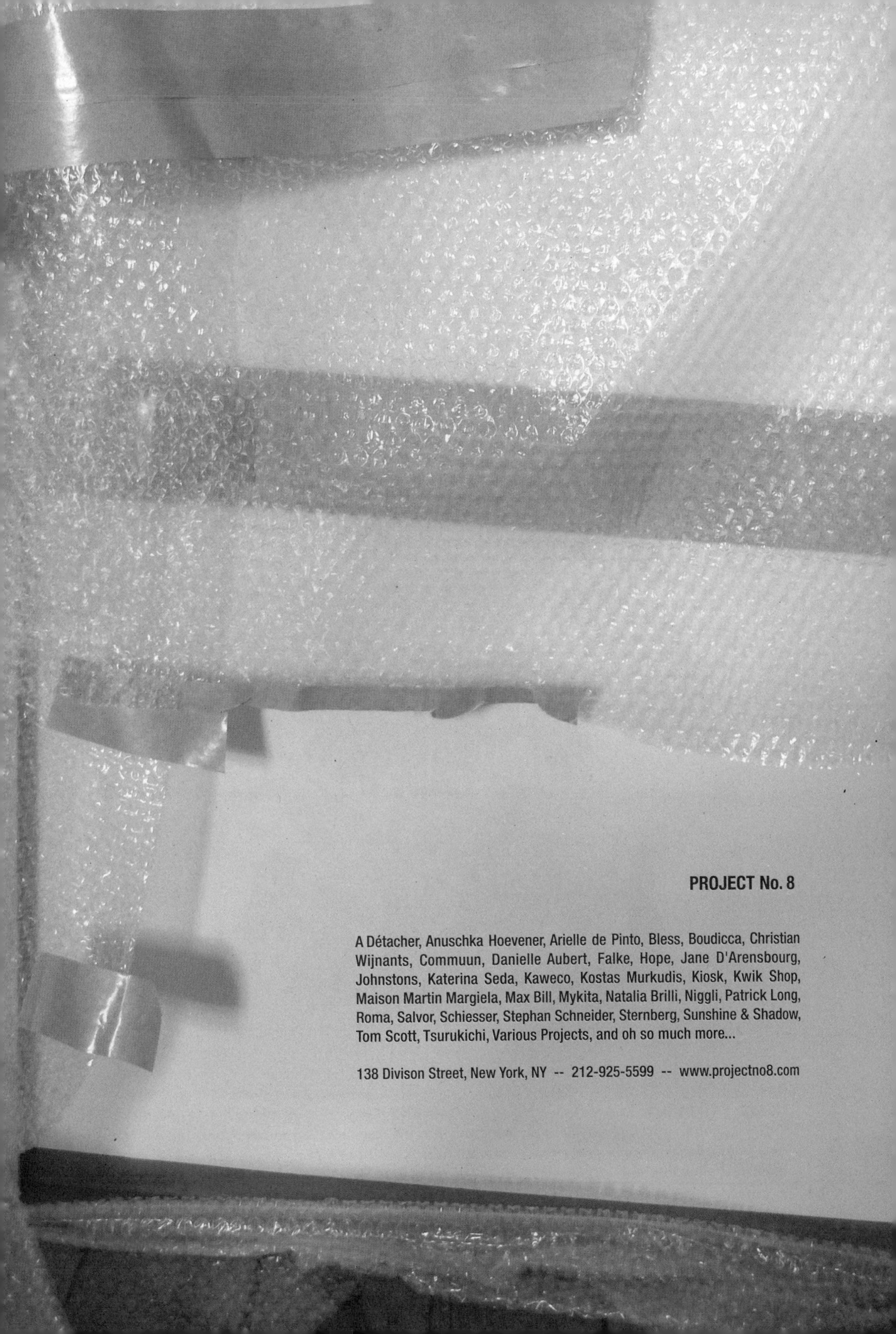
PROJECT No. 8
A Détacher, Anuschka Hoevener, Arielle de Pinto, Bless, Boudicca, Christian Wijnants, Commuun, Danielle Aubert, Falke, Hope, Jane D'Arensbourg, Johnstons, Katerina Seda, Kaweco, Kostas Murkudis, Kiosk, Kwik Shop, Maison Martin Margiela, Max Bill, Mykita, Natalia Brilli, Niggli, Patrick Long, Roma, Salvor, Schiesser, Stephan Schneider, Sternberg, Sunshine & Shadow, Tom Scott, Tsurukichi, Various Projects, and oh so much more...
138 Divison Street, New York, NY -- 212-925-5599 -- www.projectno8.com

MONSTERA DELICIOSA

PHOTOGRAPHY BY SILVIA ORLANDI
TEXT BY ANNA CLERICI

Common Name: Filodendro
Age: 12 years, with us from February 2007
Height: 2,10 meters
Water requirements: Watering and misting every week during the summer months, avoiding direct sunlight. Reduce watering, making soil dry in between operations, during the fall/winter period.

We found it in the entrance of a 70s' abandoned building complex 50km from Milan, and we carried it home on an old white Toyota pick-up. We replaced the support and the soil at the top with new ones, fertilized it and cleaned the leaves with a wet cloth. After two months, it began to grow again and so we called it "Selvaggia".

A PROTEST AGAINST DISAPPEARANCE

BY MARKUS MIESSEN
FILM STILLS BY ANRI SALA

Books, magazines, newspapers and other forms of printed matter often become part of a space and truly represent the personality of the individual or group that inhabits it. To furnish something could be described as the act of providing something, most likely a space, with a necessity. It emphasizes the idea of a service to oneself. This can be simple, utilitarian, eccentric and complex, but – most importantly – it applies a requisite, as informal or formal as it may be, to a given scenario. For most, this entails pieces of furniture, carpets, appliances, for others it necessitates careful or not-so-careful curatorial tactics to distribute visual material across their environment. To supply those necessary materials indicates a preparation.

Personally, I always found books and other forms of readable matter the most rewarding means of providing a setting to live in. Whether they are absolutely necessary remains debatable. Nevertheless, they provide an unmatched experience of accumulation, a physical and visual record of individual and collective memory. If one thinks of books as opposed to other forms of furniture, they manage to surprise through content rather than their primarily visual presence. Depending on how they are being used in a space, they might even offer structural qualities. I once visited a second-hand bookshop in Antwerp that was so stacked with books that the only available space within the entire volume was a series of narrow gangways between irregular and structurally unsound walls of books. Walking through those canyons, one couldn't stop thinking that the act of purchase would in fact cause a collapse of the whole interior as withdrawing one of the books from a stack might unbalance everything. It seemed that the most interesting 'duty' of the space was to unravel both the spatial qualities of paper as well as to unravel new relationships between books: spines as wallpaper revealing a never-ending index of memory and knowledge.

Private archives are structured (willingly or not) on the basis of exceptionally distinct habits. Whereas most formalized libraries use classification systems that are so generic that everyone can follow them, personal collections are based on eccentric logics of placement and order such as colour, spine length, thickness, size, type of content, year published, author relationships, subject matter, country of publication, publisher, spaces discussed in the book, cities, countries, languages or simply the way in which the books respond to types of other furniture or space available. On the other hand of course, books rapidly tend to become a spatial issue: the never-ending quest for new books and accumulating published knowledge exposes the dilemma of how to cope with the physical limitations of space.

In many ways, my worst nightmare are the research facilities set up by large publishing houses that require technologies such as electronic paper. To me, the idea of GoogleBooks reduces any form of written matter to pure information that can be translated onto a screen and therefore not only questions but opposes and destroys any understanding of publishing as culture. Of course one might argue that, in terms of environment and sustainability, these efforts are well worth it. And indeed, it is great news that people in the most remote corners of the planet now have access even to rare publications. However, I find it difficult to imagine where these technologies might lead us in a decade or two. I am saying this not as a nostalgic romantic, but rather from the point of view of a culture to be nurtured. And this culture to me is spatial.

As curator Hans Ulrich Obrist says, "books furnish a room". Together, we are now working on two projects that will hopefully allow us to elaborate on our ideas and optimism in regards to the culture of publishing, collecting and its spatial resonances in private and public spaces. This new movement will propagate a protest against the disappearance of books. The first project attempts to assemble a database of individuals who have serious book obsessions; private individuals, friends, and collectors, people that have noteworthy archives or simply an everyday fetish for books and printed matter. The second project attempts to rethink, evaluate and generate formats of spatial and programmatic collision, overlaying cultural, artistic, public, and residential space in a new bastardized typology in the Swiss Alps. This remote cultural centre sets out to bring together the local and the global scale on one site. In order to do so, we are investigating existing and historic utopian typologies, and corrupt, bastardize and proactively generate a toolbox for working out how to localize utopian public and private scenarios without a client: how can they be generated, followed up, and realized through active involvement in the general framework of project-making?

Central to the project, curator Hans Ulrich Obrist's personal archive and library – consisting of countless books, rare journals, interview tapes and DVDs, postcards and many other artefacts – will be turned into a publicly accessible capsule of thoughts, relationships, investigations and productive modes of curiosity. It presents an attempt to see what happens when the relentless obsession of an individual collides with the public arena. The collection is currently housed in a private flat in Berlin, packed up in Banana crates waiting to be re-activated. A key idea explored in one of our first discussions was the potential of a space activated by the archive, a space that would generate both alternative knowledge production through visitors to the library, but at the same time offer the opportunity for a long-term involvement of a small group of people through an artist residency program in a spatial hide-out. As we have now found a political partner in Switzerland to follow up this effort, we have started our investigation into typologies that will allow us to exploit the potential above. At the end of the day, the most important quality of the space will be the potential for it to become a test-ground of how space can be furnished beyond the prerequisites of walls and ceilings.

OTOMI CEREMONIAL CENTRE

BY ENRIQUE GINER DE LOS RIOS

Mexico State is characteristic for its high, yellowish and humid all through the year pasture. Pines and oaks try to break the stepperian rhythm. Factories do break it much better. There are many and whatever of these you might wish. Bread, glue, car parts, canned goods. As you go by the highway their characteristic *bouquet* enlivens it.

That enormous quantity of factories is dew to a successful government tax reduction policy during the seventies, with a clear intention of attracting the industry sector to this zone.

The Otomi Ceremonial Centre is also from the same period and the result of a government policy. A massive construction which pretends to render homage to this old prehispanic culture. "First light in our history dawn" which has become a marginal rural community.

The Centre is at more than three thousand meters over sea level. There the pasture is as yellow as it was though short and dry, and it grows in winding slopes. The pines and oaks make woods round the enclosure. The architecture is monumental in a neoprehispanic way. Huge platforms just like landing strips make you think in the possible existence of UFOs in 1976.

Another example of other culture influence are the gardens; Upon that intense yellow there is a feast of a thousand different form bushes. Walt Disney's imaginary meets the Italian *giardinetto* and some patriotic symbols. Savage horses running in circles, elegant penguins sporting bow ties, puppy dogs and even human scale jags. All of them cut out with such a skill you inevitably think of Edward Scissorhands. Many of these creations grow on circular stone basis making us remember Otomi culture is what we are talking about.

As the editor of the ultra-chic downtown fashion magazine V, Chris Bollen made what could have been something strictly to look at into something equally compelling to read. Chris gave V both heart and intellectual punch, interviewing heavy weights such as Gore Vidal, Joan Didion. Norman Mailer, Salman Rushdie and Robert Altman. Recently Chris made the move into publishing's major leagues adding his name as Editor-In-Chief to the historic legacy of Andy Warhol's Interview. His plan is to return the magazine to a place that New Yorker's will be proud of again, dumping the celebrity worship for a focus on personality. Seeing

CHRISTOPHER BOLLEN lives in a cottage in the middle of New York City

INTERVIEWED BY MICHAEL BULLOCK
PHOTOGRAPHY BY KIKO BUXO

Chris's place his own personality becomes clear, right from the unique entrance. To get to his place you walk through a womblike hallway in a turn of the century West Village apartment complex. The back door opens onto something unheard of in the city: a front lawn. In the middle of this sizable private courtyard filled with tall trees and ferns is a free standing one story cottage, a place that looks more like the home of Snow White's seven dwarfs then a dashing young editor. With this home Chris has pulled off the impossible. He created a tranquil writer's retreat in heart of the urban jungle. His outdoor picnic table is the perfect place to spend a late summers night.

How long have you lived here?
I moved here from an apartment in Gramercy in May of 2006.
I got it because my friend lived here. He had lived here for many years. I was at a birthday party, this was like early 2005, I was sitting across from him. He told me he had this amazing place, this cottage, he was saying "I think I have to move because I have so much equipment and so many clothes." He was a fashion photographer, "that I can't fit it all in anymore" So sight unseen I said "you have to make me one promise in this lifetime. If you ever leave it you have to let me take it over." It's exactly what I always wanted.

You could just tell from the description?
Just from the description. So, I was literately like a vulture. I called him like once a week for a year. Asking, so did you find a new place yet? He was a friend but not a close friend. I don't know if I ever even called him before at all. Then, he finally moved out. I was with him when he told the landlord he wanted to move and I was there right away to sign the lease. It's the only ways to get an apartment like this. You basically chain yourself to the person that was there before you.

Is it set up the same way as how he set it up?
He used the bedroom as an office and put his bed in here, (the living room) which made the whole place look so much smaller. I made it into a living room and took out the office and shoved my bed in.

Do you know what the history of the place is?
He was under the impression this was a carriage house, a staple and there were horses here and stable boys in the 1900th century. Which turned out to be complete fiction. The first summer I had a lot of people over and one night I had Chris Bram over, the writer who wrote Gods and Monsters. He lives in the neighborhood and he fancies himself something of a West Village historian.. He was very taken with this place he asked when it was built. I told him it was a stable for horses and promiscuous stable boys, of course as I said it, it sounded ridiculous. So he went to this library on Seventh Ave. where they have records of every building in the West Village and found out that the building that you walk through to get in here was two separate buildings and they were connected. The hall you walked through to get in here used to be an alley. It was connected in 1927. The same year they stuccoed the front. It was very popular at the time and it was the same year they built this cottage. I think it was basically a folly. Like it was someone's bohemian arts studio. So it wasn't for horses – and it was built in 1927. When you sit outside you realize how much it doesn't feel like New York City.

Do the neighbors use this courtyard?
No, the only neighbor uses a small corner but the rest of it is all for me.

So they can all watch you?
Yeah. And I dance for them and I usually try to break up out there and give them something to watch. It is a bit rear window meets the shining. (laughing)...
So I have been here two and half years. It's so unusual to have a house in NY.
I moved here to NY in 1996 and I think I have lived in every different type of place there is from Washington Heights, all the way to Green Point and this is definitely my favorite.
I feel so happy here. I love the West Village, although it's a little too cute for me. But this cottage is really the special part of it. It's so quite. You never hear traffic when you're here, you just feel completely away as you walk through the tunnel.

And it's magic.
It is. It's really good for writing and that is what I spend most of my time doing when I am not at work. And I want to keep it as a writing studio even when I move to somewhere maybe more livable because there is a lot of problem with living here too.

Such as?
Well for one there is no insulation in the walls so the winters are freezing cold.

Does the fireplace work?
No. I wanted to but it was going to take $5000 to clean it out.
But is this old man on the third floor... He and his lover are the kind of people that scream things like "I'm not yelling at you" they're fighting constantly, they are really great. (Laughing) One day he was out walking his dog and I said hi. He is really from a different time in the West Village, Which I love. He calls everyone Mary and stuff.

I told him I might clean out the chimney so I can light fires and he paused for a bit and stared at me directly in the face with this hard look and said, " If you start a fire all that smoke will go into my windows and there will be real trouble." So I decided not to.
So, it's freezing cold. It's like urban camping. But the biggest hazard may be that there is no closet space. So every inch of storage counts. I had to take out the stove for more room. So I don't cook, I have a microwave but it's just filled with cookbooks that I don't use. Every extra space counts. I mean it's amazing when you don't have a closet how cumbersome shoes are for example. They don't stack, you have to be inventive, and most of them are under the bed which is also nice because the ones that are out are the ones I really like .

In each apartment have you kept the same furniture?

The furniture in my last apartment in Gramercy, in fact, in the last three apartments I have had; Williamsburg, Gramercy and here are totally different, just because of how the spaces were layed out. I couldn't keep the same stuff.

So eBay everything and start fresh?

Well the Williamsburg one was full of things I found on the street. It was also when I was young enough and it doesn't really occur to you that they could have bedbugs or tics.
I was so poor when I moved to Williamsburg. I had this red velvet fold-out couch bed that I would let guests sleep on, and it was basically all springs. It was the most uncomfortable thing ever. People felt really abused when they stayed with me. So I didn't take that with me. But from Gramercy to here nothing fit. It was a long thin rectangular studio. So I bought everything long. And here there are so many edges in little rooms with so many corners... I had to change that up. So I got this couch. It's a Chesterfield, it's from Paris from the 1930's. I love it unfortunately no one can sleep on it when they stay here cause it's to short. I have always wanted a chesterfield my whole life, and I love that it is green. So that is great.

It looks literary?

Yeah, because this place could easily.... It was actually hard to get a good vibe in this place. I'm not one of those people that is obsessed with clean sterile environments. I would like it to be a bit chaotic and eclectic. But this place could easily become gypsy- like, Stevie Nicks style. One wrong batik and (laughs) and it could take you somewhere crazy. So the Chesterfield is lived in but also proper and I have a lot of art

Is it from friends?

Yeah Wade Guyton, made this little X print. See, everything has to be small cause there is no real way of attaching it to the walls. Judith Eisler drew that for me, it's a sketch from *Coal Miners Daughter* which she did. Uhm. Who else? I have this
post card from Joan Didion, she is one of my favorites. (he shows me a hand written postcard that is framed in glass so you can see both sides).

Who did she write it to?

To me, I'm a big fan of hers. This one is supposed to a portrait of me. But it really looks like a mix between my friend Drew and Hilary Clinton, (laughing) neither of whom I think I look like, at least I don't think.

You're much better looking.

Thank you.

Do you find that the art people give you reflects your taste?

I am really lucky, I don't know if this is a telling thing about me but, most all of my friends who are artists, I really like their work. I don't know if I picked them because I like their work, but I do really like it. I don't have any friends whose work I secretly hate. Or maybe if I don't like their work I just don't invite them to birthday parties, I noticed that's the real score.

You said you changed your furniture from one apartment to the next. Did your style change?

I like kind of a mix and match style but I did change it. It was much more modern at the old place. And that would not have felt right at all here. I kept the pieces I liked, but ones with little character and nothing to crazy or radical. This place has so much character on its own that you don't need to over style it.

Do you think about what you would do if you owned it?

Oh yeah, I would build a second floor for the bedroom. And have the whole first floor be the living room. That would be ideal, but not possible. I tried.

You did try?
Well I asked but it is owned by a huge conglomerate owned by William Gottlieb who basically owned the West Village. He recently died. He was really wonderful himself. For years he kept people from building, so big part of the reason the West Village looks the way it does is because he didn't let anyone tear it down. Now there are battles with his heirs. Who knows what is going to happen. This whole thing could be knocked down for luxury condos. It seems like every piece of property that has character will be maximized and turned into some glass box. It would be very sad to me if it went to a banker. Although a banker would probably not live here, it's not the most comfortable place.

Does the place affect your writing?
Yeah, because of this court yard the idea of nature comes into the book I'm writing a lot more. I even put the cottage in the book; It's owned by an old man who looks nothing like me, hopefully, and he actually gets killed in the cottage. I hope I have not written my own fate. If you find out that I am dead, you'll know to read the book. (laughing)

What is the most important thing to make a place feel comfortable for you?
I feel like it can't be sterile, the one nice thing is because for those of us who live on our wits in jobs in offices where we are moving so much, you could easily feel in NY and I have felt this way at times, like a factory worker, you know, you go home lie down get up and repeat the same routine day after day.

NY's culture factory.
Yeah, exactly, I mean their great uniforms, but I still think it's important to have the feeling that your not living in some sort of storage unit. You need the feeling of humanity in your space. I actually love hotels. I love traveling because I love staying in hotels. And I love the idea of living out of hotels.

What is your favorite hotel?
Well I always loved the Château Marmont, but that's a given

Your place feels a bit like that hotel.
It has the same kind of bohemian but somehow vital feeling.

Would that sum up your style?
That makes good sense. I never want anything to be too quirky, I don't want it to be too eccentric: It could get into madness.

What was your notion of the city before you moved to NY?
I moved here for college but I always knew I wanted to live here because my aunt and uncle lived here when I was a kid, and I would come up in the summers and visit them. They had a great

loft on 26th St in the Flat Iron district. My uncle was a surgeon and my aunt was very fashionable and fun. I would come up to visit and she would take me shopping. I remember she was trying on clothes in this store in Soho and there were all these giant Irish wolfhounds walking around in the store and I thought it was the craziest. It was the 80's and it was a decedent insane place.
It had that "anything can happen" kind of feeling. I think that's common, that's what one feels one will find in New York. I was always very attracted to it.

Do they still live here?
No they moved out in 2002. They live in Paris now. I always wanted to live here, but I have to admit I find it odd that all of us are adults and we live in places smaller than our childhood bedrooms. I mean, it's not what you dream about when you're a kid, that one day you'll live in a smaller and less comfortable place.

But who needs a big place when you have the whole city?

Well, the next place I'll live in will definitely have closets.

What do you still love about living in NY?
I love that it is all street culture, and even if that is an obvious thing to say, it really is amazing that everyone, no matter how rich or poor, have to eventually walk out on the street. You just run into anything and everyone, unfortunately less often than before because it's so cleaned up. But it's still great that you're forced out into humanity. NY is very European in the way it is built, with a small center and all wedged in so everyone has to walk around. To me that's so important for being inspired. I take the subway to work and I love it. Some people give you that look like "you take the subway, you must be having financial problems". I think the subway is so great. I love it.

How has the city changed since you have been here?
I don't know how it's changed but I think I have changed. When I first lived here I was living way uptown with not any money as a student. I remember my friend Susan and I would go downtown to the Lower East Side or the East Village. Avenue A was so dangerous then, in the 90's. We would stay out until very late because we didn't have the $20 it took to take the cab home and the subways were very infrequent at 3 in the morning. We would just stay out because we didn't want to accept the fact that we had to take the subway... And it was 7 in the morning and you were going home looking crazy and everyone was going to work and it was just like "Jesus Christ, thank God I'm really young", and I was, so in a way I feel like I have just gotten older. Sometimes the utter excitement and euphoria of living here dies and you become an older person, I don't really like the idea of being jaded but I think there is a moment when... It's like a marriage; you fall out of sexual love with it and it becomes like a companion, it's still a sexy companion. It could still surprise you maybe if it put something exciting on. (laughs) but sometimes I think of moving. I would never leave altogether but I would love to spend a year away.

Where would you go?
Right now, I really want to go to Morocco.

Have you been?
No, I often fall in love with places I have never been but I would also like to live in Paris. I actually find it hard to write in NY. That's one of the blessings of the cottage. You can concentrate and be uninterrupted but there is a very great distraction level. An A.D.D. level.

Well yeah. There is always an opportunity for instant gratification but then that starts to get soul-less.
I think there is an idea that NY is dead like it's over and not as fun anymore... well I am also 32 years old, I'm not 22 anymore. I mean how much more fun could someone possibly

eak out of their life than I already have. When you are looking to be entertained at maximum speed constantly, It starts to become tragic. And you have to give it to the kids, you have to let them do their thing and butt out a bit. I don't think I'm that old (laughing) "just wheel me back to my room. Grandma's tired now". That is something you hope for in NY, that there will be new chapters.

Well Interview is a new Chapter, has it been a big difference to go from making a magazine that is independent and sort of niche to something everyone can see.

Los Angeles because it was full of actors. And I understand it was just because the obsession with celebrity increased. I want to bring back the feeling of NY.

Well there was no living downtown culture in it.
No, none, that's why it's really great to work with Glenn O'Brien who was there back in the day and is a real New York character that has heavy roots in the city.

That is what is so unique about the situation, when businesses are bought out the goal is never to return them back to their roots.

Completely, V was really exciting because it felt so utterly new. There was really no history to it and you could invent it but Interview has such an amazing legacy, and everyone has ideas. I mean you go to parties and hear, "if I had to remake Interview this is what I would do to it." Everyone has an opinion on what Interview should be because everyone had a time when Interview meant something to them. So it has been fun because everyone is so curious and also it's a big responsibility because we want to make everyone still want the magazine. People have this idea of what it was back in the 70's and 80's and you want to return that feeling to it. And to me it felt like now it wasn't New York centric, it started to feel like it was made in

It's a really rare thing. I want to make it younger too. I think that's also a rare thing about Interview even though it is 40 years old next year. It still has vitality to it. I think it is the Andy Warhol syndrome. That's a great thing to have, people have more respect for him now. I think people that have no faith in magazines anymore still believe in the mythology of Interview and what that was and what that will be again.

What is the philosophy of the makeover?
The worst thing you can do when you take a magazine like that is to make it look exactly how it once was, because then it's just pure nostalgia. I looked at all those old issues I re-

ally pored through them to get ideas and get the feeling. I think it's about getting the spirit back in entirely new ways, ways that other magazines have not even been doing, to rethink the formula entirely of interviewing itself. I think there was a real attempt to give it a heavy emphasis not so much on celebrity but personality. Which is what the early ones had so much. At the same time Fabien Baron redesigned it completely so it doesn't really look like it recently and it certainly doesn't look like it did in the 70's or 80's but it has a cleanliness the 70's and 80's had to it.
We definitely wanted it to feel downtown. It's weird when a magazine doesn't feel like it's from the city it is from. It's really important to have the people that live in the town the magazine is made respect it most, not least. You know what I mean.

Like it became a lie?
Well, why don't you just move to Los Angeles then? I mean a magazine should know what's going on five floors below on the street. That's where I can give something and Glenn and the people we know. V was a totally different beast, but they are similar in a way because they have the idea of pulling together all different types of culture and pulling them together. So it has that similarity but it has been a blast, I am really happy. I often wondered at V, "What I would do next?" I thought maybe I wouldn't do magazines anymore. Like maybe I would do film, or be a freelance writer, I really did not want to do any magazine that I could think of, and then when this magazine came along, it was like it came out of the sky and it was just the best thing. I didn't even question it. I was absolutely sure. I mean Interview was the magazine I read when I was in middle school thinking about New York and dreaming about what kind of lives are being held elsewhere so I was excited to enter my name into that kind of legacy.

Any parting thoughts, anything heavy on your mind?
I wish New York would go through some sort of art renaissance. I think it's sad if people can't look at New York and be a bit dreamy about it. About the craziness... I am from Ohio, so I hope kids in Ohio feel like New York can be a place to be free. Maybe they don't feel as trapped as I did when I was in Ohio. Maybe New York isn't the beacon anymore because the rest of the world has eased up. Even if that is the case, I still hope New York is a promise to them, that there is still somewhere crazy left to go.

Being editor of Interview you're in a position to create the seductive signals that call the next generation to New York.
Probably we all got into magazines and the art world because we were a little bit freaks ourselves. It's likely the only business that would have us too. It's not like there were a lot of options. So those are important to keep going

They are safe havens.
Yeah, safe havens for the deranged (laughing).

www.interviewmagazine.com
www.vmagazine.com

“INDICIOS PARA OTRO LUGAR”[1] False Utopias and Identity Misappropriations for the Common... Good?

EXECUTED BY JOAN MOREY

Images from the project “Indications for Another Place” (Adrià Julià, Copyright 2008) and its investigative framework.

«Si vos sciences dictées par la sagesse n'ont servi qu'à perpétuer l'indigence et les déchirements, donnez-nous plutôt des sciences dictées par la folie, pourvu qu'elles calment les fureurs, qu'elles soulagent les misères des peuples.»
Théorie des quatre mouvements et des destinées générales, C. Fourier. (1808)

Nothing seems more remote today than the peculiar social order dreamt up by French philosopher and "Utopian Socialism" theorist Charles Fourier –those communities of individuals, autonomous as to production and consumption and based on a universal principle of harmony. Nowadays we could feasibly spend our lives recounting the times the word "crisis" appears in the media. Ours are times of mortgages turning into life sentences, and the general population gives into pressure (politically and economically) well after reaching the point of critical concern. Cities succumb to a brutal modification, a reassignation of functions and a disoriented expansion of borders. For some time now our society (even amongst theorists) has abandoned any Utopian mention when defining its goal within a complex and cumbersome urban grid, wherefrom to direct Real Estate speculation and the automated generation of benefits. Undoubtedly, fellow-man's well-being has become a missing link of sorts, disgorging into a *cul-de-sac* and lacking any resonance. And, to such politicized fallacy, "Deaf ears to ill-bearing words;" this of course, as long as the tired Government structure continues to legally underpin the right of use of property that belongs to another.

This article takes as its *leitmotiv* the developmental parameters of *Adrià Julià's Indications for Another place* a work of art investigating a mid-nineteenth century architectural project brought to fruition in the United States based on the Utopian ideas of the Socialist Charles Fourier. A group of his followers, finding themselves in a strange land, implemented his cooperative premise in their construction of Phalansteries*.

Julià analyzes precisely the history and consequences of these architectures and follows a course rendered by today's remaining ruins in the American landscape: a place that now proves unsettling, or at least perturbing, where the paradigm of "turncoat" individualism frames any and all indication of place. Surely a place removed as far as possible from the torment of "the other."

Previous page:
1. Title of Adrià Julià's Project shown recently at the Centro Cultural Montehermoso Kulturunea de Vitoria-Gasteiz (Álava, País Vasco/Spain).

On this page:
"Indicios para otro lugar". "Marcus Spring Cottage." Loop of the 16mm b&w film, projected over mural paint, reserved. Adrià Julià, 2008. Installation view.

***PHALANSTÈRE**

"Avis aux civilisés relativement à la prochaine métamorphose sociale", Fourier. (1808)

French Utopian Socialist François Marie Charles Fourier (Besançon 1772—Paris 1837) announced the advent of an insatiable society endowed with some inconceivable means to achieve a civilized order. He theorized about Utopian Socialism by conceiving a rigid while liberating community in which basically, each individual worked according to his or her passions: *Le Phalanstère*.

2

Phalansteries would be the barest of rural social units, self-sufficient and harboring diverse economic activities as well as living spaces and one large common house. They would be created voluntarily by its members, never to exceed 1,600 people living together in the one building providing collective services. Every person would be free to select his or her line of work, changing jobs as one wished. But salaries would not be the same for all. Everything would be regulated following a very distinct order, even love and sex. By keeping at the forefront of his mind a comfortable life that would in turn provide the highest amount of pleasure for the citizenry, he created his basis for a social transformation.

In other words, Fourier –more than any other Utopian Socialist– tried to solve all of society's problems via an elaborate system of social organization whereby every person, activity or thing was preconditioned to occupy a very specific place. These were theorized communities with a tendency to radically destroy the basis of current social, political, religious and family structures in order to substitute them with completely different ones. In this manner he founded the Societary or Phalansterian School.

In practice, however, only one Phalanstery experience in France became a reality, and it failed immediately. It proved too difficult to mold into reality the often convoluted ideas of one single man. The prominence of Fourierism declined rapidly in Europe while remaining well-received in America, where it earned a certain intellectual prestige. The idea of a cooperative way of life was attractive to many people. In a short while between 20 and 30 Phalansteries were created, but only 3 survived beyond 2 years. The most successful one was called *The North American Phalanx* (NAP) and it was dissolved after a spectacular fire finished off all of its assets. Beyond being riddled with intrinsic difficulties, the Phalanstery failed because of its rapid growth: in little time, it attracted a large number of ill-prepared and compromised individuals.

After his death, Fourier's ideology underwent a small reorientation. Victor Considérant (1808-1893) took over the Fourierist School and, under his direction, Fourierism became a political tool and a social movement more involved in monarchical subversion and emphasizing capitalist structure than in Fourier's anatomy of love, which had always been man's most pressing issue in civilization. In 1852 Considérant and his partisans founded the *La Réunion* Phalanstery in Texas which, after a tough and checkered life, was finally dissolved in 1854.

Curiosity:

Towards the middle of the 20th century, Fourier's ideas were of interest to various Socialist intellectuals finding themselves outside of the Marxist mainstream. After the Surrealists broke with the French Communist Party, André Breton wrote his poem *Ode à Charles Fourier* in 1947. Herbert Marcuse's Freudian-Marxist classic of the 50s *Eros and Civilization* mentions Fourier as an important representative of a Utopian hedonist tradition.

2. Portrait of Charles Fourier. H.F. Helmolt (ed.): History of the World. New York, 1901. University of Texas Portrait Gallery. Drypoint etching.

«Before there was Communism, about 40 years before Young Marx so much as proposed his first writings to "The German-French Annals" (Deutsch-Französische Jahrbücher), an anonymous source in Lyon delivered to the world Charles Fourier's The Theory of the Four Movements (Théorie des quatre mouvements et des destinées générales.) It was 1808 and the United States was young, eager, and ready for social proposals justifying its political autonomy as a nation. After some arduous 200 years of religious and political emancipation from England, a new nation was ready to absorb a lasting economic (mercantile) and mechanical (industrial) system coherent with its rebellious inception. It was a period of ideas and experiments, excitement and disillusion. With a similar spirit to that of contemporary world fairs and expos -yesteryear's multinational samplings of the most penetrating technological advancements- society was bidding for its future in conventions that publicized fresh and exciting sociological philosophies, theories and experiments. As it turns out, the inspiration would ultimately derive from Ancient Greece and the chosen model for the nation's heritage would be Democracy. But this is not the story of what has been; it is the story of a wholehearted conviction promising a stimulated, satisfied and productive American 19th century.» Thus begins Débora Antscherl's text on Adrià Julià's project "Indications for Another Place." It is a precise contextualization providing a good starting point wherefrom to tackle the artist's diligent project.

With regard to this first contexture, Adrià Julià concentrates on Fourier's followers, those who implemented his doctrines as well as his models of transcendental reform. Julià pays special attention to Victor Considérant and his sympathizers, who put into practice numerous Phalansteries in America. He centers his project on two of these: *La Reunion* in Texas and the *North American Phalanx* (NAP) in New Jersey. The artist, submerged in an enthusiastic voyage –in search of any trace of this willpower to create a Utopian urbanism– gradually fleshes out an ample investigative frame by closing (or formalizing) his project with two categorical films installed according to complex indications. The pieces –entitled *"Marcus Spring Cottage"* and *"La Réunion"*— invade, sequester and reinterpret all vestiges or new conversions remaining of the above mentioned Phalansteries; or rather of how they have fallen into oblivion, vanished into the landscape or been absorbed by today's American society.

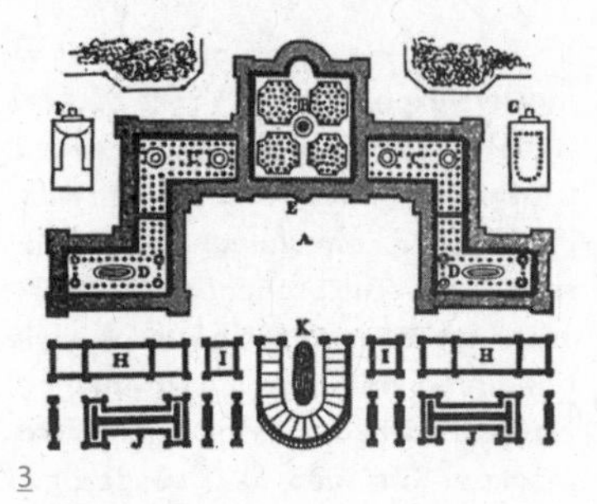

3. Sketch of a Phalanstère model projected as the ideology of Fourier. Author unknown.

Opposite page:
Press release about the spectacular fire which destroy The North American Phalanx (NAP). Article published in the newspaper ASBURY PARK, N.J., 1972.

Thus Adrià Julià has created an expository assembly based on some of the formal ideas explored in Charles Fourier's visionary eccentricity, as well as on how his theories remained latent as a literary, philosophical, poetic and linguistic phenomenon. In turn, the path prescribed for the space occupied by "Indications for Another Place" finds the viewer surrounded by an almost mystical sensuality. Although, at certain moments –especially opposite the *"La Réunion"* piece– incomprehension or rejection were to set in through some of the action filmed, since both image and sound are in slow motion. This bears a clear deconstruction of any direct bond to the Phalansterian aura, with Adrià Julià bamboozling the audience with an enigmatic and obscure phantasmagoria of allegorical incidents.

"Indications for Another Place", as pointed out by Débora Antscherl, adds interpretative layers to Fourier's already complex socio-aesthetic conversations. In spite of the multiple readings already associated with the signifiers' system of Fourier's legacy, Julià conducts a psychological exploration of the language. It is his way of confronting a discourse previously probed in his older work: "A Way of Passing the Time" (2007,) "Truc Trang Walls" (2006,) "La Villa Basque" (2005) or "Anatomies for a Common House" (2004.) He has already analyzed these themes and syntaxes of the social treatment of collectivity, of Utopian objectives, de-colonization and contextual re-adaptation as well as the multiplicity of facts that intervene in the formation of the individual as a social subject or as a thinking individual. He devotes special attention to the analysis of "representation" and its insertion into architecture or landscape.

ASBURY PARK EVENING PRESS

ASBURY PARK, N.J., THURSDAY, NOVEMBER 16, 1972

Phalanx Fire Followed by Sorrow and Anger, No Clues

COLTS NECK TOWNSHIP — As firemen and police continued to investigate the fire which destroyed 80 per cent of the historic Phalanx House early yesterday, persons connected with the 123-year-old structure reacted with sorrow and anger.

Monmouth County Fire Marshal Leonard Mack was unable to determine the cause of what he termed a "suspicious" blaze which consumed much of the house before firemen arrived shortly after 11 p.m. Tuesday.

State police at Colts Neck said a specialist in investigating arson cases would study the ruins of the house today to search for traces of chemicals.

The police said they had no leads on suspects.

The owners of the house, James B. Casey and John Smith, both local businessmen, visited the site about 3 p.m.

As falling snow caused steam to rise from the still-warm embers, the two men walked slowly around the structure, shaking their heads and occasionally testing a wall or foundation.

Mr. Casey, who purchased the site from the Monmouth Museum this summer, declined to give any immediate plans for the remains of the building.

From the road, the Phalanx resembled a Hollywood movie facade, with the front of the house almost intact while behind the front wall nothing remained but heaps of charred bricks and timber.

The fire destroyed the three-story portion of the building, leaving untouched

ago and then — after the university admitted it had no funds for restoration — donated the site to the Monmouth Museum, yesterday charged the two institutions with gross neglect.

"If I had known they wouldn't make a better effort to restore the house, I never would have deeded it over to them," Mr. Blackburn said. "I feel so terrible — I think now I could have gotten local people to raise enough money to have done it ourselves."

Mr. Blackburn owns about 180 acres to the south and west of the Phalanx site, land he has owned since 1949.

"I really think it was inexcusable for both these groups to let it fall apart," he said. "During the last few years, nothing was done. They didn't even bother to board it up."

Severe vandalism during recent years had reduced the Phalanx to a shell, with the loss of destruction of such items as "the three mahogony staircases, which Hollywood offered me a lot of money for several years ago, but I refused," Mr. Blackburn said.

In California, architect-writer Dolores Hayden said she was "very, very sad" to hear of the fire, saying that in the U.S. "there is nothing else comparable" to the historical significance of the Phalanx.

After traveling to the Phalanx a year ago while researching a book, Miss Hayden almost single-handedly aroused the interest in preserving the structure.

She said the North American Phalanx, which was or-

Colts Neck Township residents look over the wreckage of the 123-year-old Phalanx House which burned yesterday morning. (Press Photo)

"Buildings reflect ideas about society and how people want to live," Miss Hayden said. "The Phalanx showed that its people thought very carefully about how they wanted to live together.

"Because of this loss of ideas, it means much more than to lose a building with simply a nice facade," she added.

Lee Schiller, president of the Colts Neck Historical Society, which had been negotiating to purchase the Phalanx site up to the time of the fire, said last night a decision whether to continue efforts to buy the site will be made "by this weekend."

He cautioned however, that "to rebuild it would not be to preserve it. It loses its charm."

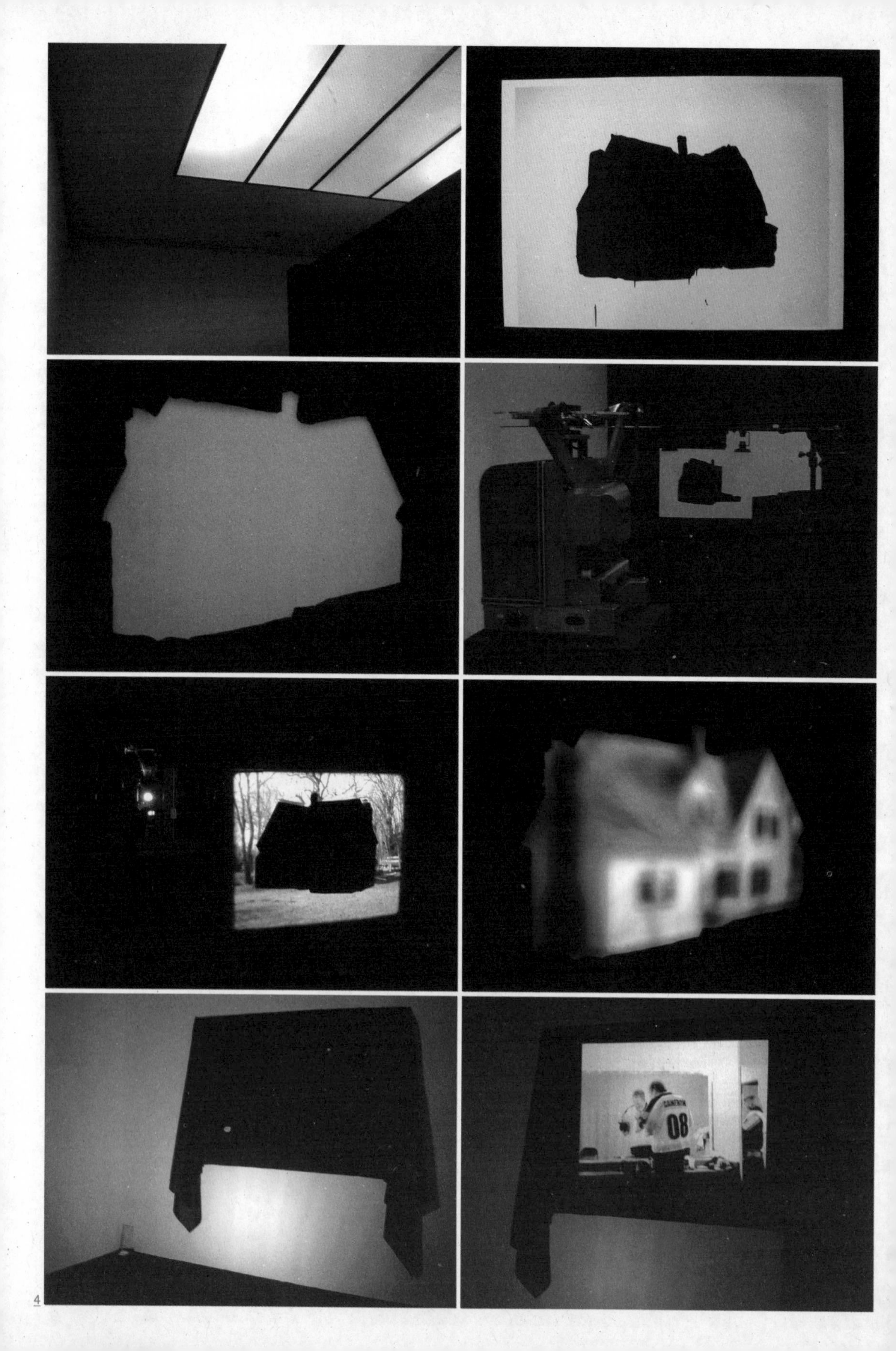
08

Adrià Julià was born in Barcelona in 1974. He studied fine arts at the University of Barcelona, but his concerns –far from the expectations that are placed on artistic discipline– drove him to expand his field of action far from the stagnant structure of Spanish education. In his search for experiential novelty he first opted for Berlin, until the city became an idealized destination or an escape valve for a large turnover of creators. This massive emigration sought to find a gap in the complex, non-sustainable state of Art or creation. Nowadays these propositions continue cohabitating in the city in an almost obsessive manner. The German capital is an epicenter where thousands of creators catch a glimpse of a Utopian *espoir*. Perhaps this equips them with a particular internationalization, or perchance a "cultural" survival is simply more economical from within an indomitable artistic precariousness. In 2001, in the midst of this commotion (which more than announced Berlin's conversion into a hotbed of cultural oversaturation that the metropolis would find itself incapable of taking on,) Adrià Julià moved to Los Angeles, where he lives and works today. There he continues his studies in CalArts (California Institute of the Arts) as a grantee from "La Caixa" and with no other intention than to prolong his artistic endeavor freely and without so many erroneous interferences.

With the calmness and *savoir faire* that characterize him, he went from cohabiting in the spotlight of a rowdy creative excitement to residing in a country where the artistic reality travels down some very different avenues. Evidently, Adrià Julià was not in pursuit of the American dream. He was rather searching for a secluded spot wherefrom to develop his concerns, transmit his ideas –mostly through Contemporary Art–, strengthen his intellect and fight the eternal battle to maintain his productive energy alive.

His previous piece, *"A Means of Passing the Pime"* was selected for the Lyon Biennial (2007) and shown at *LA><ART* (Los Angeles, USA,) the *Generali Foundation* (Vienna, Austria) and at *Galería Soledad Lorenzo* (Madrid, Spain.) Julià's solo shows in the last few years include venues such as the *Anne de Villepoix Gallery* (Paris, France,) *The Room Gallery* (University of California at Irvine, USA,) *Artists Space* (New York, USA,) *OCMA* (Newport Beach, USA,) Sala Rekalde (Bilbao, Spain,) Espai Zero1 (Olot, Spain) and *Palau de la Virreina* (Barcelona, Spain.) Through his many group shows Julià's work has traveled to Los Angeles, San Francisco, Pasadena, Austria, Lisboa, Oldenburg, Berlin, Bremen in Germany and several other art spaces in Spain (Madrid, Barcelona, Santiago de Compostela...).

www.soledadlorenzo.com

04-05. "Indicios para otro lugar". Adrià Julià, 2008. Installation views of the pieces entitled "Marcus Spring Cottage" and "La Réunion" during the assembly of the exhibition.

5

IGGY AND THE STOOGES
RAW POWER

East Village Downtown

PHOTOGRAPHY BY CARLOTTA MANAIGO

I live in the east village. The building is fun, because there is a mix of young and creative people and old peculiar folks who have lived here since the hippie and crack years. They could all be charachters out of a book by Salinger.

There is a lady who sits in the lobby holding a fan, a guy who smokes like a chimney late at night, he calls me Mussolini just because I am Italian and when I try to talk to him he says his mother adviced him not to talk to strangers.

He must be 85 years old. Then the guy downstairs who plays some exotic instruments and whistles along, and the grumpy successful art photographer who dries his socks in the stove. He took my portrait on my last birthday.

Inside, my apartment has more of a Parisian atmosphere. The light is magical especially in the afternoon, which is great for pictures.

I look out to nice trees and a fountain. Its pretty empty still, decorated with vintage furniture, my tv hasn't been connected yet and is lying on the floor while I still listen to records.

I am particularly proud of my miracle octopus plant growing in the kitchen. I am babysitting a puppy these days, he loves to jump on my white couch and eat my socks.

Its a nice place to hide away from NY chaos.

The Camelot Solution

TEXT BY MARCO VELARDI
PHOTOGRAPHY BY MARCO VELARDI & FELIX FRIEDMANN

We heard about Camelot for the first time when Yorgo Tloupas, Editor-in-chief of Intersection magazine, visited Milan last April and told us about how incredibly cheap his rent in London, was £60 per week, while living in a beautiful huge building. Shortly after we realised it was not just Yorgo's case but a sort of incredible community of individuals living in such exceptional places as fire stations, schools, castles, council offices, and who knows what, across five countries: the Netherlands, where it all started, the UK, Ireland, Belgium and France. The more we spoke to friends and people around us, the more we began finding out incredible stories and experiences about Camelot, both good and bad. Curiosity grew even higher, but at the same time realising it would have been unrealistic to pursue a 360° view on this phenomenon. Taking a personal approach to it was the only way forward. Invited by Yorgo, we took a trip to London last July to experience the Camelot style of living and, while being there, we briefly met up with photographer Felix Friedmann who told us about what life in an ex library feels like.

www.camelotproperty.com

YORGO TLOUPAS, is a 33 years old, half French half Greek, art director who moved to London from Paris 7 years ago. He founded Intersection magazine together with Dan Ross and Rankin, after working for Crash and Magazine, further developing it into an international publishing empire made of four editions in Japan, USA, France and Dubai, with two more on the way in Germany and Russia.

Were you originally based in France?
I was born in Paris, and I always lived with my parents, in the leafy suburbs. My father, Philolaos Tloupas, designed and built his own house in which I grew up and I still retreat to when I travel back to Paris. He drew the plans and built it all by himself in the late 60s late 70s, with just one other guy helping him. The house is actually pretty amazing, and it has been featured in various design magazines. It is a very minimal open space structure designed around the ancient Greek golden ratio, which is supposed to make the proportions perfect to the eye, with big windows, totally white and no curtains. To grow up in a house like that, unlike any of my friends' ones, has always been the normal thing. Only later on, I realised how truly lucky I was to grow up in such a situation.

Do your parents still live there? Have you got any siblings?
My parents still live there, and there is no way I would ever give the place away. I have also a sister and she is living in a place my dad worked on, he took an old farm, and he redid the inside for her.

Has he built other houses then?
Not really, he is a sculptor by trade, literally he built those two in France and he did something in Greece for our own house over there. He built an extension in the shape of a minimalist block of white concrete with sleek windows, attached to this traditional looking mountain house. It is a very interesting combination!

So when you moved to London, leaving behind these beautiful houses in the country, did you already know about Camelot?
Not at all, I didn't have an idea about Camelot seven years ago. I first moved into quite a cool place, called the Golden Lane Estate –www.goldenlane.co.uk–, which is next to the Barbican, built by the same architects. It's a listed building with a very utopian structure, big windows, and strongly influenced by the work and ideas of Le Corbusier. I moved into a studio with a small garden by my own, because I was not sure about sharing a house, like everyone does in London, as in France kids live mostly by themselves. I still remember it was so expensive, £800 a month, and I lived there for 1 or 2 years. Afterwards, I moved into a live and work (loft) space, with a separate room for my bedroom. Basically, I was living in the magazine's office, which was great, but it became difficult to keep the place tidy, and suddenly there was no more space for my private life, as well as I ended up working non stop.
Before I began living with Camelot, I spent some time with two friends, who were living in a similar type of place to the ones Camelot provides. It was 400sqm for £200 a month near the Barbican tube station. They were super great set designer, working on the Vivienne Westwood catwalks installations, music videos and much more. The building had a workshop downstairs with a massive courtyard that was never used. Another floor was used as their storage, while the upstairs of approximately 150sqm was where we lived. They built everything themselves, like the whole kitchen in one day, then they separated the whole floor with partitions. Our bathroom was covered up in prints designed by Eley Kishimoto, as we are all good friends with them, while the walls of my room.
My room walls were made out of shoeboxes, since one of their friends was a shoe designer, so we had these cardboard that would contain 6 shoeboxes each. In between these we put some of the light boxes you see here at my place now, which were remaining from some music video, could be even a Madonna one. The whole thing was freestanding, no tape, I loved it! The rest of the place was an extravagant mix of Victorian and modern, both very messy and very eclectic. Unfortunately, we got kicked out after a few months, but we kind of knew it as it was a dodgy deal. After I moved out, I found out one of my employees, Bjorn, was living with Camelot already, so I tried to get a place too.

What's the deal to get on board with Camelot?
There are definitely a few prerequisites in terms of about who you are and what you do. You can't be a student to move in, you can't organize parties, have a cat, or smoke inside.

They will let you stay as long as the locations are available. And the move out warning is just one month.
Normally, it is quite difficult to get on board. You have to fill in an application form and you are put on a waiting list, but essentially you have to convince them to trust you. In my case, I had the email of a girl working at Camelot and after writing back and forth a few times I managed to go and see her. At first it felt like I would not be able to get any accommodation, then after 10 minutes, she suddenly told me there was a free room in a school in Chelsea. Literally, she gave me the keys and I took my bike and went to see it. It was the right one for me, so I took immediately.

What was it like?

It was a fairly similar location to the one where I live now, a sort of art and design college, but it was totally abandoned. I think they temporally moved some people out of the building before I moved in, so the kids from the estate nearby began smashing things and doing graffiti. Things went back to normal right after, so I felt quite happy about the whole Camelot system, to stop squatters or people to vandalise the properties.

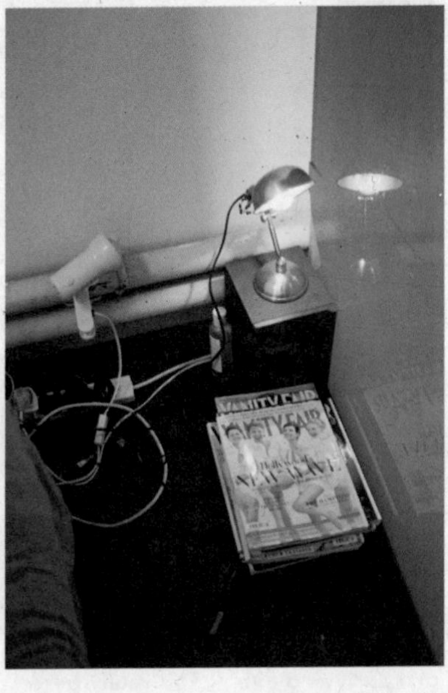

Well, then what happens on the occasion you have to move out?

If you have been good to them, like paying rent on time and respecting the rules - you are given a set list of rules at the beginning of your tenancy -, they will propose some other venues, and you can choose from those. I went through the whole process when I moved out of Chelsea last Summer in 2007. They proposed me some other rooms, one of them was in Felix's school, but it was too small and not the kind of space I wanted, so I put my things in storage and waited. What I like about Camelot is the big spaces they offer, like Felix has got. In the end, I heard about a new school with empty rooms, and I knew a girl who just moved here, so I asked Camelot and it worked out. When you are lucky enough it works really well and they are efficient.

I wonder if it's all based on word of mouth or is there a forum or bulletin to find out about the available properties?

They don't show properties on the website for security reasons, to prevent against squatters. The practice is that they email you proposing to show new places every now and then. I actually got one offer last week, but it was far outside London. You always hope that isn't the venue they propose you next. I could not live outside central London.

How many places do you think they manage in total?

I have no idea, but they have venues all over the UK. To be honest I know most of the people would want to be based in central London.

How does it work with the standards they provide such as security?

There are a few basic things for living you get guaranteed such as fire extinguishers, a common area with a fitted kitchen and a shower/toilet for example. You can also add your own things like a washing machine. On the bad side, I have also heard some properties don't have heating, but I have never been into one though. As for security, you are supposed to guard the place, there's a whole set of guidelines. Honestly, it is quite easy even though it always depends. Right now I live next to a council estate and nothing has ever happened.

Do they give you any furniture?

No, but for example in my case all you see fits into a van, and in takes 25 minutes to put it in.

Do you have extra storage space somewhere?

I had books, but I keep them at the office or I took most of them to my parents in France. I love books but the idea of moving them around was driving me crazy, mentally and physically, so I am avoiding any, beside a few small things I can easily carry around or leave at the office.

Do you buy furniture then?
Not really, lately I only bought some Muji cardboard boxes, which I use as my closet. I normally find things around and got some from Habitat, when we first launched the magazine as we did a deal with them. Those cardboard boxes are great, you buy them flat and can easily carry wherever you want. Regarding some of the rest, the couch is a Robin Day reissue from Habitat, I really like his 50s' designs. My dad built the table; it is such a heavy one, while the chairs are Habitat again.
Ultimately I prefer classic things and build mixes of own and found stuff.

Anywhere to check for inspiration?
I quite like the blog Dzine. I also love how people manage to integrate cars in their houses, there's a magazine called Garage Life from Japan, where garages become part of the house or office with similar fixtures to the actual car interiors.

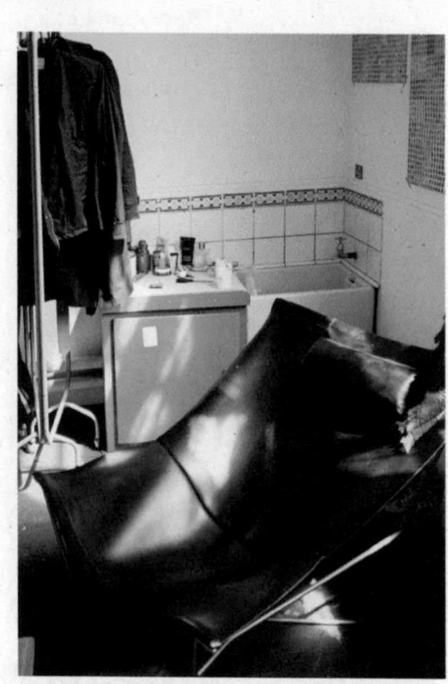

Going back to Camelot, do you think it is something many people know about?
If you start talking about it at a party or a dinner, someone will know for sure, but it takes a bit of courage to live in this kind of situation, where you could be evicted within a month notice. It's almost like you play a lottery. You leave the living side of your life to chance, I mean you can choose but not everything. It's probably the opposite of what most people do.
So you perceive of Camelot as a community?
It is just a house sharing, it is cheaper and more bohemian.

How do you feel when you come back home, knowing it's not going to be permanent?
I don't have a TV or radio, if I had a screen to watch videos I would like it more. My real home is in France and Greece. I like Saturdays when they are quite, and love coming back here and cycle in the courtyard. Living here is a good test to bring girls and see how they get used to the basic things, like for sharing the bathroom. One thing I miss is to have cats, but you are not allowed.

Do you think you could quit this type of living style?
Well with the kind of life I have, being always on the road, travelling a lot, if I had to pay normal rent it would be frustrating. After tasting something like Camelot you don't want to start paying normal prices. It is ridiculous. On top of this I don't know even how long I will stay in the UK. It could be that I move back to Paris at some point.

Camelot just launched in France?
Yes, it is just happening now. If it works out, it will solve lots of housing problems. I am also looking for something like Camelot in New York, as I thought of moving there. I don't want to pay crazy prices. It is not picking up even if it is full of empty buildings in various areas of Brooklyn, such as Greenpoint. When you start living within the Camelot frame of mind, you begin to look at spaces in a different way, already thinking how it could be used. You really become aware of the possibility of transforming state owned spaces or abandoned buildings into temporary living situations. The aim for any organisation trying to do so, it is to find the hole in the loop. Whether it is more expensive to pay 24hr security guards or having temporary tenants taking care of it.

Have you already thought about the next step?
My next step might be prefabricated housing, or even an airstream trailer, the big American silver ones, and place it on top of a car park. Prefab houses are amazing. I have been looking at this website –www.prefabs.com–. I don't know why it doesn't take off as a concept. But I would like to explore the possibility in NY, to rent a parking space in a car park and try if it works.

PUT
LEARNING
FIRST
ROOM

Swiss born photographer, FELIX FRIEDMANN, grew up in a small town in Austria and spent about 10 years of his life in Vienna before driving up to London in 2003 with his girlfriend Arlette. Introduced by Yorgo, we met with Felix and Arlette in a London bar to chat about their experience with Camelot.

How did you find out about Camelot?
Frank van Delft, a Dutch friend and photographer had been living with Camelot in a care home in Crystal Palace. In October 2006 he moved away from this far south London area to the a new central London school property called Lilian Baylis. A couple of months later, he told me that there was more space available and hooked us up with the Camelot office and recommended us.

How did it actually work for you? Were you given a choice of places? Or you had only one option?
A week after signing up with Camelot we received a phone call saying that we could move into the same school as Frank on the same day. We were pretty lucky and got only this offer, which was what we really wanted.

Was it easy to get hold of the library? How many people live there?
When we got the first viewing and the available rooms were shown to us, we were told that the library was taken, so we decided to take over two classrooms, but they were not half as great A week later, at the second viewing, everything was different, the previous couple moved out because of winter temperature, which was quite weird. Well, it was finally available and we got it! I think the capacity of the school is around thirty people.

How is it living in a library? How was the place once you got it? Did you find the original furniture inside?
It is the greatest place I have ever lived in and I guess it will not be beatable in the near future. There was nothing in there what so ever. 180 totally empty square meters, 90 downstairs and 90 upstairs.

Do you have your own kitchen or is it shared? How about the rest of the facilities? Do you have inside rules between the different people sharing them, like do you have meetings to organise the cleaning schedule?
Luckily, we have a dedicated small "kitchen" room upstairs. The others don't have that and because of the fire regulations they are not allowed to cook inside their rooms so they need to go into a common area with a shared kitchen.

In terms of meetings we don't really have any. Common sense should help living together in harmony. So far it worked out quite all right, beside the hair in the shower sieve. I could have already made a wig out of them!

I got the sense when you are with Camelot things are not totally stable, as in one month you might have to leave your place. How do you find living with this uncertainty, do you consider your place like home or more as a temporary condition, therefore never losing that sense of hominess?
I consider it our home 100%. We appreciate it everyday. I admit that living like this is almost a form of religion to us. Sometimes it gets funny when the council, who is the owner, turns up with architects to discuss future usage. We panic for half a day and then we calm down and start being believers again. Obviously we would love to stay as long as possible and when the day of moving will eventually come, we will do so with great memory of Lilian Baylis.

What is the best and worst part for you of living with Camelot?
Being allowed to live and work in a 180sqm space in central London, which is very quiet with trees, green spaces, foxes and singing birds. There is no bad part, but to answer the question maybe the growing wig.

Do you see yourself using Camelot for a long time or it is only a temporary phase?
When time at Lilian Baylis will be over, we will see what happens and in which state of being Londoners we will be in.

Would you ever consider getting a place of your own without any of the Camelot conditions or you think it is not worth it in London?
We have lived in a south London flat before Camelot and it was a dull, horrible, noisy and dark hole. To be in London was great enough, I guess. Living with Camelot is definitely living within certain rules, quite easy going though, but I can imagine at some point in the future there will be some contradiction for us. That being only one rule: no kids allowed.

The Carneys

PHOTOGRAPHY BY YE RIN MOK
TEXT BY ELSA FISCHER

Jewelry designer Marti Heil and her three musician children, Reeve Carney, Zane Carney, and Paris Carney all live here. For twelve years this has been their home. It's my dream house and a tribute to the American dream. A place to meet and be met with open arms. A place to inspire and be inspired. Alive and yet with energy to live. In a world where nothing is quite as it seems this is a sanctuary of togetherness. A fairy tale. Part dream world, but all real. Alice in Wonderland meets now. A Home.

When I asked Marti Heil about her home it all started as a conversation on space. Then it became the story of how grandmother Heil met grandfather Heil. A search for old photographs. Sweden. Memories. My Life. My conversation with Reeve began with the two of us trying to ride his bicycle. Reeve always walks on the car side of the pavement. He mentions wood. He makes me taste chocolate cola. They were both meetings with people that are truly reflected by their home. Extraordinary, warm, beautiful and welcoming.

I felt I couldn't add any words to explain them better.

I love the Carney children. I love their mother. Their grandmother, and I love their home.

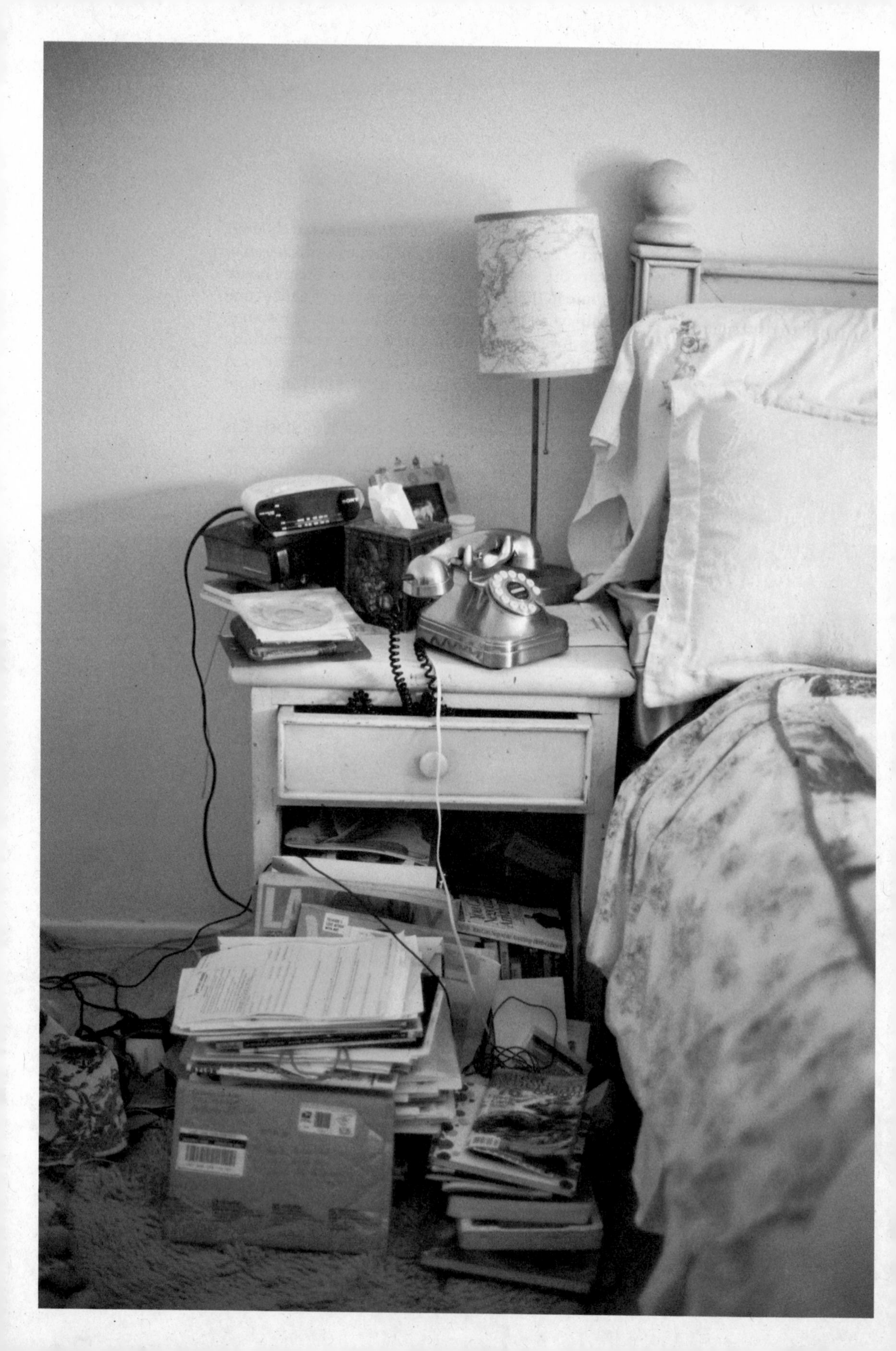

DAVE'S WORLD
NEW!
MONDAYS ON CBS!

SANTA

JULIAN GATTO
Growing roots at home

INTERVIEW AND PHOTOGRAPHY BY JUAN MORALEJO
TEXT BY JULIAN GATTO

My girlfriend Mercedes and I have been tendering plants for about a year now. I would say she specially likes succulents and cacti, while I like ferns and moss. But what we have come to realize is that we like combinations- not only of plants, but of plants and the object or container that houses the plant. So throughout the year each container has it's "moment" -when all the elements come together at a certain time, making the pot more beautiful than it ever was before. These days we are getting strawberries from one of our pots, so it has become a favorite.

We also like adopting weeds and plants we find in the streets. So many of our plants were taken from other places and have grown roots at home.

Julian Gatto is an Argentinian artist, renowned for his multidisciplinary enthusiasm. From carpentry and botany, to sketching and tapestry. Having learned through trial and error rather than through professional means, his chaotic home doubles as a study, where his projects are allowed free reign.

How long have you lived here?

Since 2006. I graduated in May of that year in New York, returned to Argentina, was looking for a house and I liked the neighbourhood.

How would you define it?

It's out of the centre. It reminds me of Avellaneda where my grandmother lived. It's quiet and suburban. It's a pace that I like from life.

Did you make any changes when you moved in?

No structural ones. Everything I did was focused on the furniture, as there was hardly anything here. I made some tables, the library, shelves, and chairs. I made the bed for the cats because when I put the food on the floor the ants always came in and the cats wouldn't touch it, but if it's raised then the ants don't find it. I got hold of some poplar wood, which is cheap and knocked it together.

Did you know anything about Carpentry beforehand?

In Cooper Union, where I studied there was a workshop. And in the last show I did there I made my own supports. So I knew a bit, but the very basics. I learned how to nail and glue things together. I like it when you can see how something is made. When it looks like anybody could do it.

And you also salvage wood and furniture from the street.

I like cast offs that you can reuse... giving new life to the things that people throw away.

Is that taste ideological or aesthetic?

It's a bit of both. I have to admit that I like seeing things that seem worthless, used.

I remember the show you did in Little Cakes in NY, with objects that were in your grandparent's basement.

There was a bit of nostalgia involved there in reascribing value to an object that had been forgotten. I also liked that the materials used were different to those used today. Even mass produced objects had a different quality about them.

But you've also got a lot of stuff from Muji in here...

apartamento - Julian Gatto

apartamento - Julian Gatto

Whenever I go to Japan I bring a lot of their furniture back with me. I think that they make the most of the materials they use. They don't hide what it's made from, don't paint them. I also like things that don't carry a logo. In some way I think it's similar to generic objects I find here in hardware stores and pound shops. I studied graphic design and I'm sick of design. I prefer it when things don't impose themselves. It's the old argument over whether design should be functional or decorative...

Let's talk about the nursery you built on the terrace.

With everything I made, including the furniture I wanted to bring plants into it. And it interests me more and more. My girlfriend knows a lot about plants and gardening and we wanted to grow plants and create an element of interaction between the plant and the structure that contains it.

Which don't have to be pots?

No. They can be found objects, or broken things that we've stuck back together but can't be used anymore in the kitchen for example, but are perfect for a plant. This isn't something unique to us – I think a lot of people do the same. The nursery has been a process of trial and error. Last winter quite a few of the plants died and we realised that they needed special care. So we started swotting up on the subject, and now we try to make sure that the fertilizers we use are organic. Recently we came across a mineral called *Tierra de Atomea*, which kills the insects without harming the plant. You can even eat it.

The other day I heard someone use the term *Avant Gardening*. It sounds like marketing speak – referring to the use of the organic as a fashion thing.

I guess that's always going to happen, that the market ends up trivialising certain terms. I think I've always had fairly utopian ideas, but I think it's important to think that way.

You recently opened a space near your house called Canasta with some other people. Tell us about it.

I stumbled across Canasta walking through the neighbourhood. It's changing with the people who are involved in it. Sometimes it's a gallery, at other times a bookshop or a workshop. All of the furniture is movable so it can be reassembled in various ways. In some way it all fits together. I suppose that identity grows out of chaos. It's the same with plants.

The Villa

BY MATHIAS STERNER

In time at need, there have always been people in my life who has come through for me. So also the people in "the villa".
"the villa" consists of 6 struggling artists all in their mid 20s.

The small house is located in the north-eastern part of Stockholm. A neighbourhood packed with lawyers, doctors, other upper-class people, and so us. This uptight crowd, supposed to be our neighbours never seem to get us, not for the lack of trying. I guess they frown upon our existence, since in their eyes we're just a bunch of rebellious youngsters moving into their neighbourhood uninvited.

The house was built in the early 60's and has not yet been renovated, which is ridiculously obvious from the outside. The owner is intending to tear it down to build a complete new house, so maintenance is not top priority. Add a badly maintained garden and you'll have approximately 700squaremetre surface that you simply can't miss in a neighbourhood so polished, that the people are competing in having the best cutting grass. Not that they're actually competing, but this is one of those areas were people never actually talk to each other, just silently judging. Picking their best moment to rub something in others faces.

At first I didn't think much of the idea to share a place with several others. In this case it was not different, although I sort of already new everyone living there. We grew up in the same town but never used to spend time together. Soon it felt like the most certain thing in the world living there sharing everything.

My friend Sebastian was the first person in today's constellation to move in to "the villa". He and his former girlfriend Ida was looking for a calm resort where they undisturbed could rehearse with their bands. It's not a big house, but they've managed to create a small space for that usage.

It's nice to have this exchange in experience when you live like this. Not the sexiest housing ever, but still it's priceless when you're having all these cookouts, or gather around for a friendly game of football in the garden, even when they rehearse, then there are people from all over country coming for a weekend of intense music playing and beer drinking.

They came through for me when I was desperate and had no place to stay, and that makes them nothing less than amazing.

This goes out to:
Sebastian, Gustav & Ida.

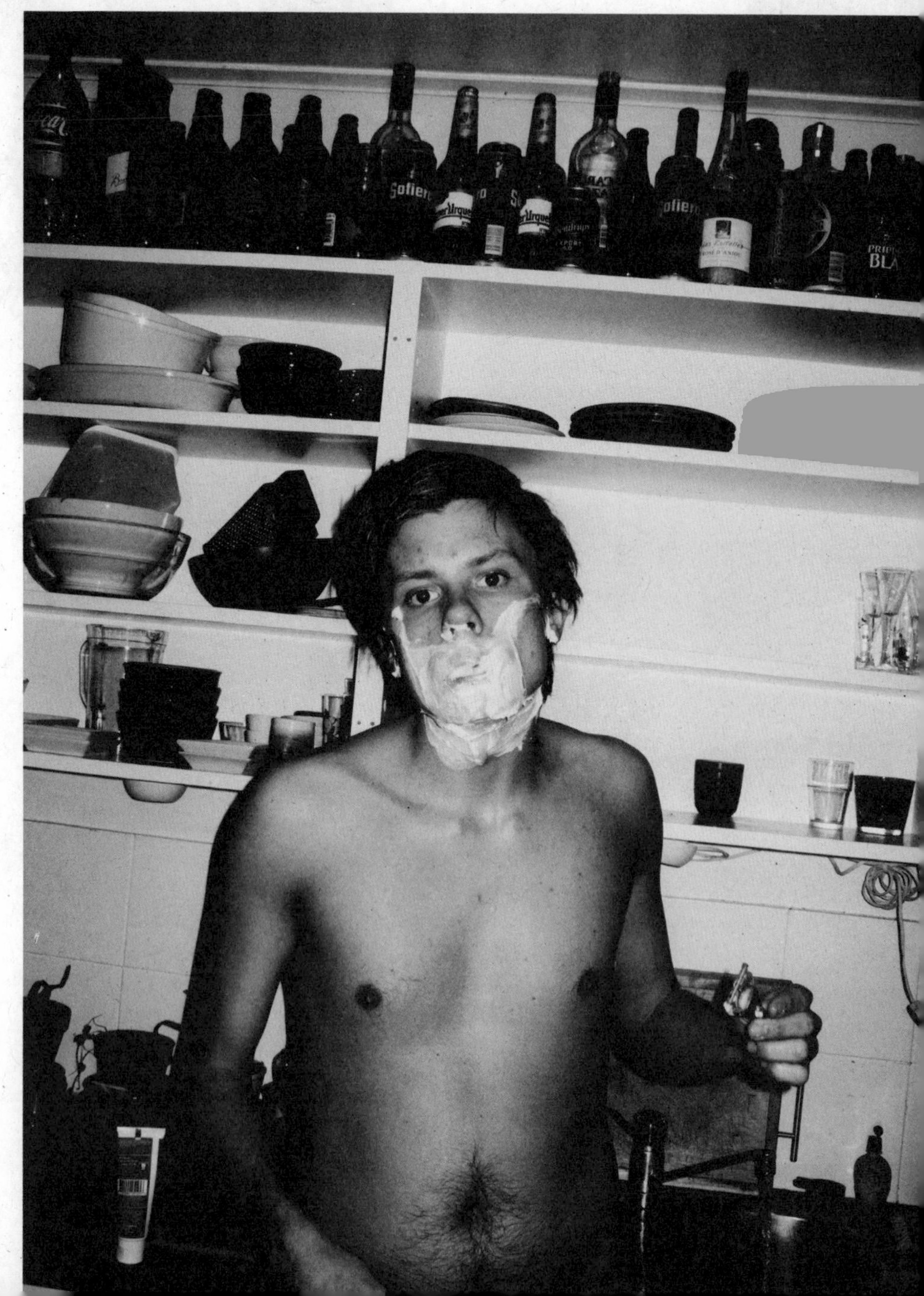
Sofiero

EROL ALKAN
At home

INTERVIEW BY KARLEY SCIORTINO
PHOTOGRAPHY BY NACHO ALEGRE

Erol Alkan first got people talking back in the late 90's when his signature mash-ups put him on the forefront of the bastard-pop wave of music. Since then he's become one of the most respected and exciting dance music DJs in the world. From 1997 to 2007 he was host to the now legendary London clubnight, Trash. A mecca for kids looking to hear the best indie and electronic music, in its ten years Trash saw bands like Yeah Yeah Yeahs, The Rapture, and Klaxons play it's stage. Most recently, Erol has taken his magical hands to producing, working with rising indie bands Mystery Jets, Late of the Pier, and The Long Blondes. But what does Mr. Alkan do when he isn't busy keeping kids dancing? Well, to be honest, he's a pretty chilled-out, sensible guy. Seated on the leather sofa of his north London flat, there's no, like, coke or sluts lying around. On the contrary, Erol's house (which he shares with his beautiful wife of three years, Chandra) is his much valued sanctuary in his otherwise hectic life.

As you walk through the front door, one of the first things you can see hanging on the wall is a piece of art that reads "the music sounds better with you," in brail. It kinds of sets the tone for the rest of the house (if you can read brail). Upstairs lies Erol's musical domain- his studio. This is where he does all of his top-secret musical experimentation. Well, one would have to assume anyway. There is an entire wall dedicated to storing his ridiculous record collection. The wall opposite displays his collection of vintage synths, acquired from different places all over the world. You can find some cool Trash memorabilia lying around here as well. Classic and beautiful, Erol's house is clearly an extension of his undying love of music. This is probably why he likes to spend so much time there.

Do you know much about the history of your house?

I know it was built in 1850, and that it's a rare example of a house in London with a butterfly roof. I actually remember being in the place where I live when I was a kid because it was a grocery about twenty years ago.

What's the most important thing you need to make your house feel like a home?

I think it changes with age. When I was younger it was the convenience of where it was. I lived on a main road above a shop for five years. It was amazing because it was close to buses and the tube and I could stumble out at 5am and get a sandwich from next-door. Now that I'm older I care about space, light, how quite a road is, and little things like the direction of the sunshine into your garden. How I wake up in the morning pretty much dictates how I am for the rest of the day, so the atmosphere in a house is very important.

Is the idea of a home being a sanctuary something that's important to you?

If I'm totally honest, up until a couple of years ago I couldn't have cared less about stuff like that. I think I was in a different mindset. I thought of my house more as somewhere to sleep. But when you start spending more time at home and enjoying your time there more, it naturally becomes something different. You start to consider every gap or blank space. It's about surrounding yourself with things that inspire you.

You travel a lot. Do you miss home when you are away?

Oh, all the time. Traveling didn't use to register anything for me, but now when I'm away I really miss home. It sounds a bit childish to say, but I get homesick really easily. When you finally find a place that you are comfortable in you're going to miss it- especially if you are in hotels all the time. I don't like hotels. For me there is no difference between being in a five-star hotel or somewhere run of the mill. It's just the fact that I'm not at home.

Is there something in your house that you are most proud of?

I'm really proud of the floor. I helped design the color and the texture of it. It's really cheap wood but we treated it in a way that makes it look really amazing and expensive even though it's totally not. But I've been banned by my wife from doing DIY now. I nearly killed myself about three years ago. I was trying to install coat-hangers and I was drilling into the wall below the electricity fuse board. I drilled into a lead and I just went flying across the fucking room. It was so scary. Now Chandra won't let me change a plug or go anywhere near a screwdriver.

www.erolalkan.co.uk

Estrella Damm
PRIMAVERA SOUND'07

The Orphaned and the Adopted

1

PHOTOGRAPHY BY ALBERT FOLCH & OMAR SOSA
TEXT BY ANTONIO MONTOUTO

After passing through innumerable homes, each with their own unforgettable memories, 've now got a little piece of each collected ogether in this space. In the past, when my apartments got too small, I lent out a lot of my possessions to friends for safekeeping. Now at last, in Ensanche, these objects tell my story rom their homes in the rooms where I pass each day. I'm lucky in that I live very close to where I work, and so I've created a salon atmosphere for my friends to come to, and a space where I can come up with new ideas for Vincon's windows. Comfort is the most important thing for me – I don't want to fill my house with items of hi-design, whose only value is in he price tag. I feel more comfortable with old, mix-matched, found and second hand items. 'd hate to feel uptight because something got dirty, old or happened to break. I love the improvised rhythm that these unfinished houses attain over time, and the feeling that they're always happy to adopt another orphan into heir fold.

. These chairs go way back. They might look ike they were worked out simply by an ironmonger, but for me their design is almost perfect. 20 years ago I came across them at a street market and fell in love with them on the spot. I went to get some money out and when got back, they'd been sold. I felt so frustrated, ike someone who's missed out on a once in a ifetime opportunity, but to my surprise a month ater they were sitting in the house of one of my best friends. It was as if they were waiting for me to sit on them. I told my friend about what had happened and 20 years later I inherited hem: fate brought them back to me. The lamp sitting on the Vincon marble table is a find from a flea market in Villanova. It cost 10 euros!

. I wanted to create for myself a spiritual space that extended through the house and he rooms. The egg carton shaped paper lamp hrows little dots of light over the wall. It throws out constantly moving reflections

. Part of the living room is given over to a small art collection. Each one of the paintings has it's own story, and some of them belong to my friend Gilberto's collection. It's a collection hat started growing with my own works, and inally with the passing of time, came into his riend's hands. Thanks Gilberto.

4. It's made from marble and has a coolness about it, which brings to mind an old-fashioned doctors surgery. Nevertheless, this little bedside table with its lamp on top is exactly wha I needed to go with the bed. I found it at the same time as the bathtub – in my favourite and dearly missed, city centre shop

5. Despite not being a loft space, the house ha that feeling about it. The living/sleeping spac attracts a soft light throughout, during the day The bed was an amazing find. I was looking fo an iron frame bed and I went to see a friend o mine who's an antique dealer. He gave it to me at a real knock down price on account of it's unusual width – 1.35 m. Thanks for that!

6. This gas stove is a fixture from past houses and still works. The bird cabinet is an old wardrobe that my mother lined to store herbal tea and I keep to the tradition. The fridge is coatec with black methacrylate, and I added some olc trunk handles.

7. I once went up to see the doorman of my building, who has a roof terrace, and wher I came down again I was carrying this little rusty blue chair. The addition of a steel worktop and Vincon handles to an old Formica table is my own touch. I like how it fits in with the other pulled together bits and pieces in my kitchen.

8. The basin is actually from the men's changing rooms at Vinçon. It spent many years watching the employees get dressed before finding it's way into my hands. The poster of the boxe is by America Sanchez and there are a fev half empty paint tins hiding in the corners. The house is, as ever, incomplete.

9. This wardrobe was a sad sight when I founc it abandoned on the street. It was a rainy day and, waterlogged, it was doubly hard work getting it home. It's missing a couple of drawers and in a past life medicine cabinet from a surgery. Even though it's still injured, it makes me feel better. The bathtub was a prototype fo an English company and has been rented ou for lots of films. It's porcelain, and not particularly comfortable. But still, it's a one off.

MARTINI
3

SUPER

5

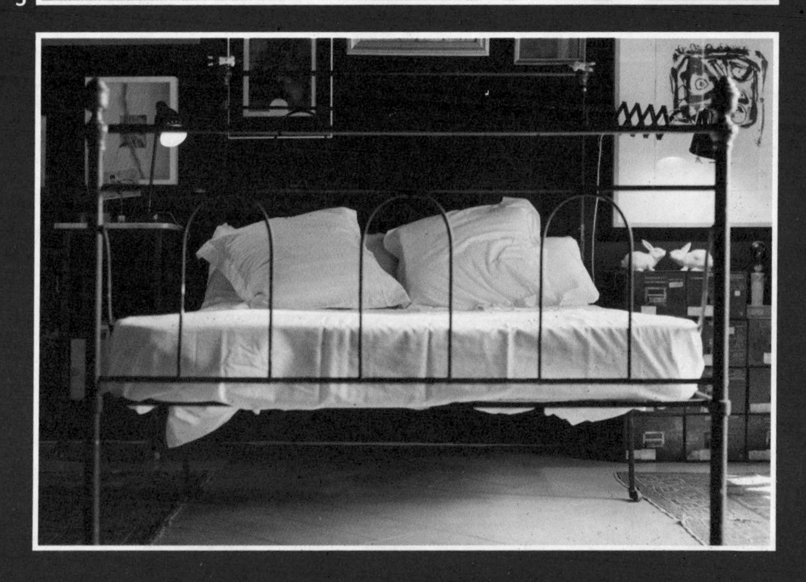

CAJA

9

MAX LAMB
Bringing material to life

TEXT BY PAULA YACOMUZZI
PHOTOGRAPHY BY MARCO VELARDI

Knowing how to be patient has been one of the keys for Max Lamb finding the place of his dreams. He now lives in a workshop converted into an apartment, on a former North London industrial estate. It is an area that is obviously deprived and ethnically very diverse. The estate is a small one; a central street runs for some 50 metres between a jumble of flats and workshops. Max shares a small, open-plan space with his girlfriend. The flawless white of the walls explodes at this hour of the day, when the midday sun shines down through the large skylight a floor higher up. Functional and bare, everything has the simple, sensitive warmth of North European minimalist industrial décor. Even the floor is a bright grey, so some of Max's own objects, and the Eames chairs around the table in the sitting room, stand out like jewels against a clean cloth. The workshop in the adjoining room has been temporarily converted into a storeroom, but its structure is still clear and tools and workspaces can be made out.

It seems as if the *Apartamento* team have come to meet Max and visit his apartment like a small army of nosy-parkers. "Marco was here yesterday, we talked about the project for *Apartamento*, and I think he wanted to take a look," Max says with half a smile which suggests that he finds our weakness amusing. But I suspect he is also flattered that his life arouses this curiosity, and because he is proud of his home, which he has created with his own hands, just like his designs. A day after Marco Verlardi's visit, I arrive, and sit on his black, polystyrene sofa (the only two-person sofa he has produced; an object that is aggressive to look at, because it looks so rough, but is soft to the touch and comfortable to sit on). We talk easily, accompanied by coffee and biscuits, while Max continually fetches objects and samples which help explain his past and on-going projects, ideas he is considering and the materials he uses.

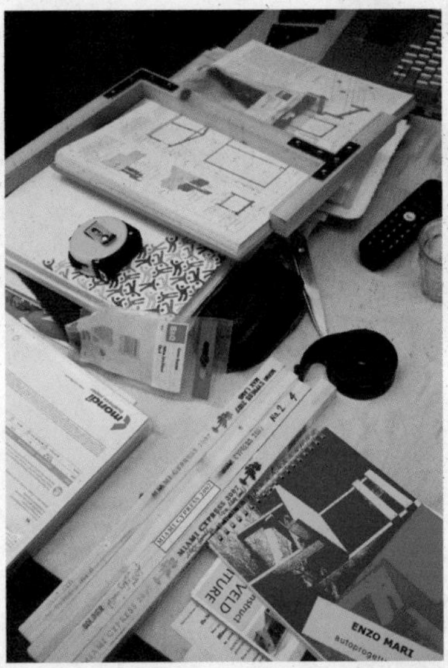

Max Lamb is 28 years old, and in 2008 was named Designer of the Future by Miami/Basel Design, where he launched his Solids of Revolution, stools made of ultra-light cement and felt. In 2006, he completed an MA in Design Products at the Royal College of Art. Over the last few years he has exhibited throughout half of Europe and the United States, won prizes for innovation in furniture design and spent a couple of years working with Tom Dixon. In 2008 he has given classes at ECAL in Lausanne, and has seen his first design for Habitat in the shops. He has also has been working on an infinity of ideas that seem to live peacefully together in his brain, without threatening to close it down. However what brings us to him is not so much his CV but rather the chairs, benches, stools, armchairs and tables that he has created. His "projects" as he calls them: sometimes as crude as chunks of nature; at other times more refined, but still just as imperfect and in all cases with a visceral and atavistic attractiveness. We are also drawn by his working methods, which combine the rigour of industrial processes (both traditional, and cutting edge) with the ingenuity and viability of handicrafts and even championing DIY; his exploration of materials and techniques as a creative and aesthetic base; his focus on the process more than on the finished product; and an approach to communication that includes filming the construction process and, sometimes, installations featuring these videos and the chance to "try out" his work.

This was the case with Exercises in Sitting, his RCA graduation project, an exploration of some thirteen ideas which resulted in seven designs for seating. For his final exhibition, Max arranged the chairs and stools in a semicircle in front of a small table with a monitor on it showing videos about the construction of each object. But he has filmed all his works. There are videos on the internet showing him turning polystyrene for his series Polystyrene, melting pewter on the beach to make his Pewter Stool or sanding cement down for the forms of his Solids of Revolution. This is the method that he uses systematically to show his work, and differentiates him not just from artists who have occasionally filmed some of their work (Richard Serra, for example), but also from a growing number of contemporary designers who have a similar relationship to materials and processes (and here I can't help thinking of Hella Jongerius). Why this approach to communication? "Before I even made any of my projects I had an idea of how I wanted to exhibit myself. Maybe following the idea of what kind of exhibition I didn't want, a very shy exhibition to show the finished object. It is all about letting people into a secret, how you can communicate, more than 'this is my design, my aesthetic and my perception of the future'. I put the focus more on the process than on the finished object."

It is the same spirit that animates his imperfect works, riddled with constructional details, whose design stems from the interaction between the materials and the actual potential of the

GB

ROBERT LUDLUM
THE BOURNE ULTIMATUM
AA Gill is away
Curious BOYM
SPOON
Philip Pullman
LUNAR PARK
Presentation Techniques
ECAL
JAMES BOND MOVIE POSTERS
Designed in Germany
GRAPHIS PRODUCT DESIGN
THE SAS SURVIVAL HANDBOOK
THE VALUE OF THINGS
New York Interiors
DESIGN≠ART
symbol soup
MARTIN PURYEAR
ROGET'S THESAURUS
ART AT THE TURN OF THE MILLENNIUM
ZADIE SMITH
THAILAND
CHRIS RYAN
Graphic Design for the 21st Century
Future Shock Alvin Toffler
GRAPHIC DESIGN NOW
CITY LIVING
THE PHOTOGRAPHS
FURNITURE MAKING
ARCHITECTURE NOW!
London Interiors
New York
Vietnam
West Africa
India

techniques. In the Pewter Stool the grains of sand that made the mould are clearly visible. We bring one out as we discuss it: it tempts one to touch it. While the surface that is exposed to the air is taut and shiny, the legs are rough and uneven, and the moulded pewter is covered in holes and grains. Similarly the structure of his Copper Stool – whose design evokes wax as a material, natural honeycombs and the research of Buckminster Fuller – shows the marks of the wax and the sophisticated processes of electroforming with which it has been moulded. His Polystyrene series cannot hide the powerful nature of his craftsmanship; it is clear that the material used for the Starch Stool comes from extruding biodegradable materials; and the Rusty Sheet Steel Chair does not just show the oxidation process to which the steel was submitted but also its cutting with a high-precision tool such as a laser. "It is the honesty of the object itself, so the object becomes almost like a story or record of the process, and you can see visual details that describe the process." For his clean, minimal designs, Max counterpoints a concept of crude beauty: "Designing is generally trying to disguise these kinds of construction details in a way. Everything's got to be hidden. I agree with that but also think that there is real beauty in the raw details. So I prefer to celebrate the beauty of the construction methods or the materials. Let the details be, rather than designing for an aesthetic."

Recently he has produced a small table for Habitat based on his Pewter Stool. The prototypes had to travel between India, where the factory is located, and London, where Max inspected the samples. It was the first time that he has been involved only in the design aspect, and he found it difficult to imitate industrially the perfect imperfections of a product that was originally made by hand. "I think we have six samples, and every one ignored a particular detail, and then I had to redraw it, focusing on that particular detail, and then they would forget other details. Maybe it is almost impossible to do, so we finally decided to let it go straight, and that would look better, because at least they will achieve a more consistent object. So it is very interesting how this thing turned out. Exactly the opposite to other things that I have produced."

A CULTURE OF OBJECTS OF VALUE

Max has now dug up a copy of a 1973 magazine titled "Create your projects at home", a type of DIY manual with instructions for building garages or erecting fences or putting up shelves. It also explains how to construct a chair out of fibreglass, using a mould. "This is amazing! If every single family uses all this material to make a mould, it is a bit crazy, they would have a whole street full of moulds!" We laugh. "And then they would have the same chair."

We have entered the terrain of Do It Yourself. Max discovered DIY when he started trying to produce his own work and saw how impossibly expensive everything was. So he started thinking about using DIY, even in the context of industrial processes, such as for the Pewter Stool. "The word 'sand' made me think of sand-casting, which is an industrial process used in foundries. So I went to the beach and made my own mould on the beach. And that's when I thought: rather than making a solid mould, a patron, which makes every single object identical, by carving into the sand directly I can make the same object six times and each one is going to be different. So that was working with a very industrialized process but using it in a hands-on way." His Pewter Stool is probably the object that gives the most complete idea of his concept of crafts-industry-DIY. But there are many facets to the concept. One of them is this project which he gives *Apartamento* so that everyone can try it at home, using simple, cheap materials that are easy to get hold of. "It engages people in the actual process of making it, which is what I dedicate my life to doing. I think this is what lots of people do. There are so many handy people out there, making their own work! I think we need to encourage that."

We talk about all the people who make things and who, for generations, have devoted themselves to making things with their own hands. We start discussing the idea of this kind of culture which, even today, to a certain extent is rooted in modern life. "Although the reasons we make things now are perhaps different to those of previous generations," Max thinks. With the same interest with which he dissects industrial and craft processes, or rummages through materials to work out designs, he analyses the mechanisms of our world of value and consumption. "I think now it is a reaction to a kind of loss of identity. Objects now are so cheap in the shops, really, scary cheap. And the problem is that everything becomes so fashionable, so transient, and these objects shouldn't be temporary because they still have a huge amount of material investment. Solid materials, metal, plastic, wood... And because they are so cheap they have no inherent value and become disposable, far quicker than their function is lost. So they get disposed of and then another one is bought, and then it gets disposed of and then another one is bought..."

So, in his view, there are two options for generating (and surrounding ourselves with) objects which have value. "One option is that you have to make something expensive so then people have to question themselves, to make a decision: if they will buy it in the first place, and then if they want to keep it. And the other way is trying to make it yourself. My parents still have little things like Christmas decorations that I've made. So every Christmas my mother shows it to me saying 'Do you remember this?' 'Yeah, thanks, Mum!'" He laughs. "So you make something and all of the sudden, though it is incredible shit, you love it. It has an incredible value! And that value is amazing, this sentimental... I think sentimental value is so important. Things that you can pass down to the next generation. Not only that an object has to have a quality that allows it to exist for several generations, real good quality of workmanship. But also it has to have some kind of sentimental value..."

He is also seduced by the exchange of products and services, or bartering. "I've made this and you've grown tomatoes, so we would exchange the chair for some tomatoes," he laughs. "Well, something like that. In fact, he has started to work on an exchange with the clothes brand Blaak, which will soon open a new shop in London. Both produce almost unique pieces, which are therefore expensive. So Max will construct furniture and they will contribute their models. With the added dimension that, in this way, they will start a relationship. "The kind of relationship that used to be so important in society, in life. That way we might become friends", Max enthuses.

Max Lamb is both sensitive and rational at the same time, and talks openly about his memories of family and childhood and the geography which contains and stimulates him. His mother studied art and occasionally painted. He remembers evenings of social events and tea with painters. His father still works for the Royal Air Force. But when looking for antecedents, he mentions his maternal grandfather and spending summers at his farm in the county of Yorkshire, or God's Own County, as the English call it, thanks to the greenness of countryside. "My grandfather was a scientist, but he retired into farming when I was almost 4 or 5 years old. So he also designed and built his own house, two houses actually, one that my mum grew up in. He was one of the most practical people I know. As a child and teenager I spent all of my holidays at the farm with him, just making things. Building my own dry wall using sand and bricks. This was my entertainment for the day, doing so many practical things. I would be casting driveways, driving tractors, doing all the farm work, hay bale dens, searching for buried horseshoes or glass bottles or making a tree house named Tremonk."

Similarly in his native Cornwall, on the southernmost peninsula of Great Britain, there is an infinite source of inspiration, with rocks like raw lumps of metal, its moorland vegetation and a past of pewter-smelting that has marked its history and its people. Max looks for and finds a photograph from his childhood, taken on a beach in Cornwall, the same one where he recently constructed (and filmed) the Pewter Stool. In the picture, he is five years old, wearing swimming trunks, his longish hair bleached the coppery blonde of a childhood summer. He is holding a plastic spade and has just dug the tunnel which you can see beside him. The 28 year-old Max laughs. He says that he has always been a builder.

www.maxlamb.com

DIY chair by Max Lamb

PICTURES AND TEXT BY MAX LAMB

The DIY Chair has been designed to be constructed using very cheap and basic building materials readily available from your local DIY (do-it-yourself) or hardware store, using simple hand tools and joinery methods, by you. I would like as many people as possible to have a go at building their own DIY Chair.

The material I have used is called 'Smooth Planed Pine' which is a type of softwood commonly used by the building industry and has a smooth, splinter free surface. The size of the wood is 34mm x 18mm and available in lengths of 2 metres or 2.7 metres. I bought seven lengths of 2.7 metre pine. Hopefully you will be able to buy the same size and type of wood from your local DIY or hardware store. The most important size is the 18mm x 34mm cross-section of the wood as this dictates the width and depth of the DIY Chair and also the spacing between the seat surface and backrest slats. Depending upon the standard dimensions and availability of softwood in your DIY or hardware store, a second option is to call your local timber merchant or saw mill who will definitely be able to offer you wood with the exact dimensions. This can be a surprisingly rewarding option enabling you to select your favourite type of wood from a plethora of soft and hardwood choices.

In England, where I bought my materials from, the wood and the screws required to make one DIY Chair cost just £9.77. Thus it is possible to personally construct a dining setting for eight people for less than £80. Of course the more the merrier. The point is, the DIY Chair is a piece of furniture that you can construct yourself, sit on and be proud of.

01. Tool list: tri-square, ruler, sharp pencil, fine tooth tenon or panel saw, sand paper (180 grit is perfect), cordless drill, 3mm drill bit, countersink, cross-head screwdriver, and 124 screws (4 x 35mm).

02. Using a pencil and ruler mark a line on the first length of wood at 47cm.

03. Place the tri-square against the edge of the wood in line with the pencil mark and scribe the line across the width of the wood.

04. Carefully cut along the pencil line with the edge of the saw to the outside edge of the line, making sure you hold the saw vertically to ensure a square edge.

05. Sand the edges clean to remove splinters. Repeat steps 2-5 until you have a pile of 31 identical pieces of wood, all 47cm long.

06. Position two pieces of wood at right angles with the wide edge on top of the narrow edge, and use the longest width (34mm) of a third piece as a measuring guide.

07. Use the tri-square to check the two pieces are at 90° and ensure the lower piece of wood is still 34mm away from the end of the top piece of wood.

08. Hold the two pieces of wood steady and drill two vertical holes next to each other evenly spaced apart, approximately 25mm deep. Then countersink both holes.

09. Screw the two pieces of wood together. If possible, set the clutch of your drill so that it automatically stops when the screws are tight.

10. Rotate the two joined pieces of wood so the lower piece stands vertically. Place a third piece overlapping the other two ensuring its end is flush with the edge of the vertical piece.

11. Drill, countersink and screw the third piece of wood, as in steps 8 and 9. Repeat through the face of the vertical piece of wood to form a perfect triangle with 6 screws.

12. In a similar manner, join a further two pieces of wood to the opposite end of the third piece of wood.

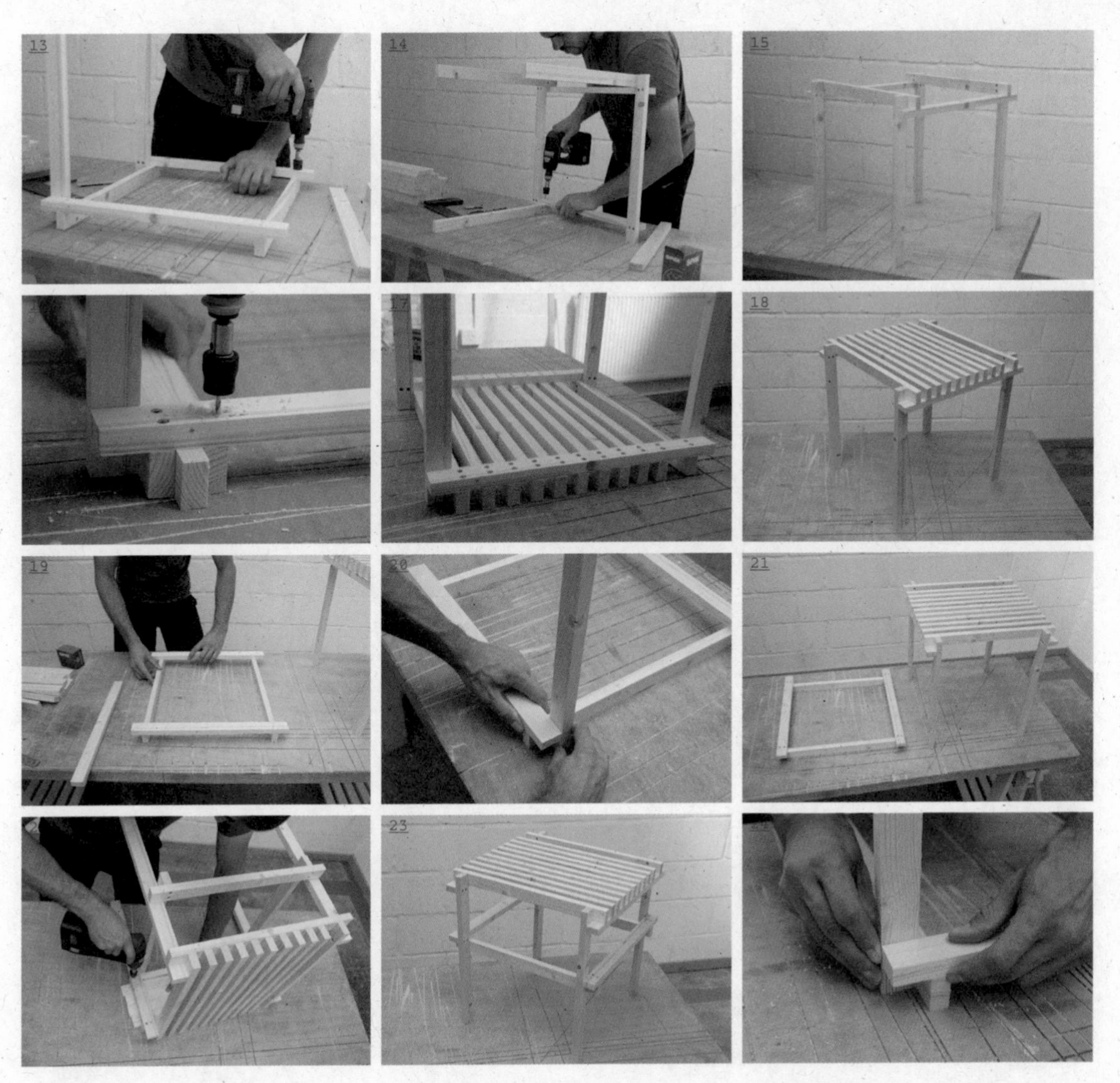

13. Drill and screw a sixth piece of wood at the opposite ends of the two parallel horizontals to create a square frame, ensuring a 34mm gap remains at the end.

14. Two additional legs can be drilled and screwed to the square frame.

15. You should now have a square frame and four legs consisting of eight pieces of wood and twenty-four screws.

16. Flip the frame upside-down and using a spare length of wood as a measuring guide, drill and screw another piece of wood parallel to the front edge of the frame at both ends.

17. Repeat step 16 eight more times leaving the last remaining gap free.

18. Stand the frame upright and you should have a total of eleven slats across the top surface of the frame. This is the seat of your DIY Chair.

19. Create a new square frame using four pieces of wood. Place the two lower pieces on their thin edge and the other two adjacent on top on their wide edge.

20. Use a spare piece of wood as a measuring guide so the two upper pieces overlap by 34mm.

21. Using eight screws, join the four pieces of wood together. Remember to check they are at right angles.

22. Slide the frame up the legs of the original frame and use the width of four pieces of wood as a guide before drilling, countersinking and screwing the frame permanently.

23. Sixteen screws should be used to attach the support frame - two screws though every wide edge of the wood - four per corner.

24. Begin the backrest. Repeat steps 6 & 7 to create a right angle with two pieces of wood. The upper piece should overlap the lower by 34mm (the wide edge of the wood).

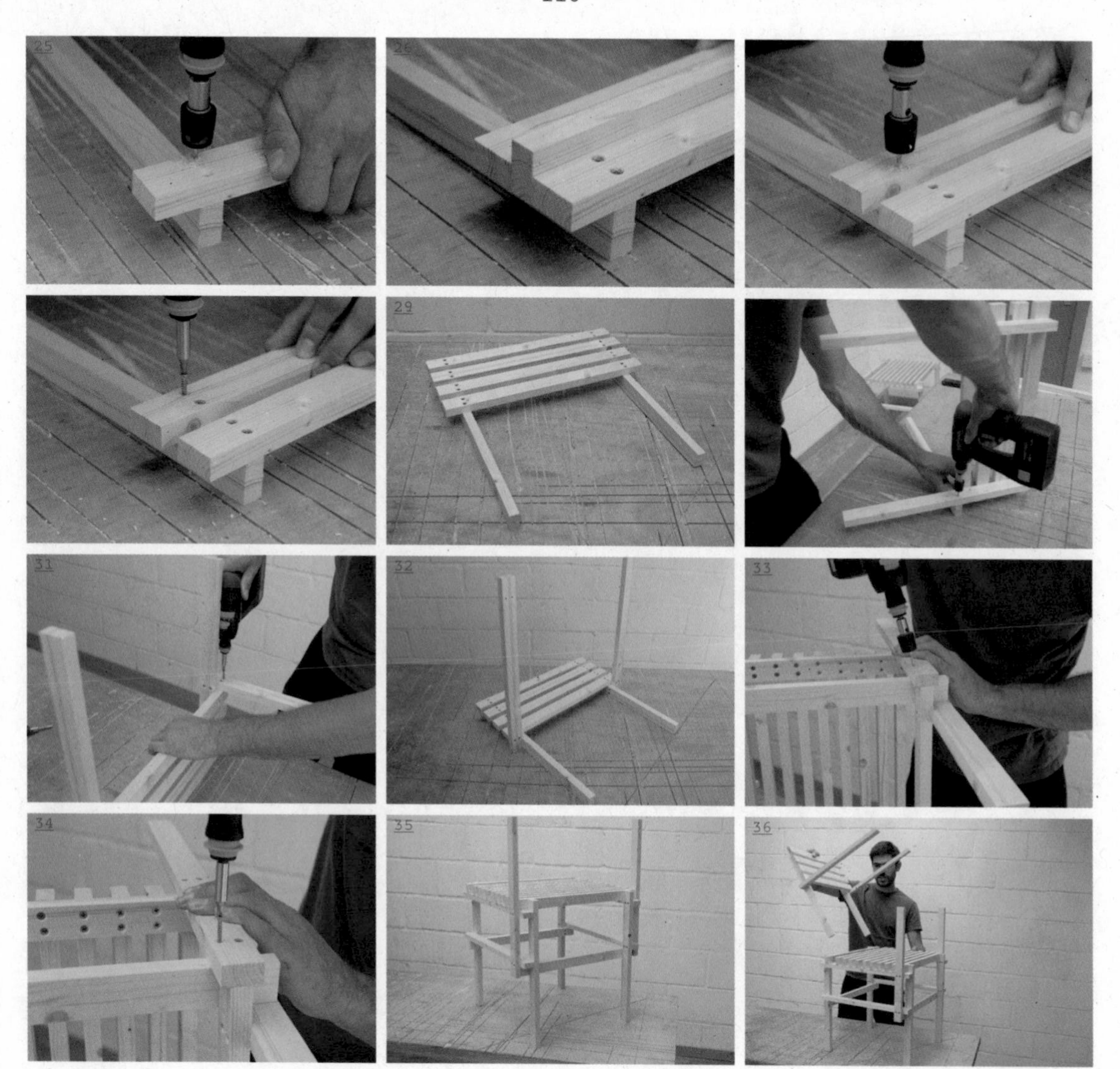

25. Drill, countersink and then screw the two pieces of wood together. Place another piece of wood on its thin edge at the opposite end of the upper piece of wood.

26. Place a second horizontal across the thin edge of the lower pieces of wood and use the narrow width (18mm) of a spare piece of wood as a spacing guide.

27. Hold the second slat in position whilst you drill and countersink.

28. Screw the second slat in place and then repeat steps 26 & 27 twice more.

29. Your backrest should have four horizontal and parallel slats in total.

30. Flip the backrest onto its side and add another piece of wood for the right armrest. This should be placed directly beneath the lowest backrest slat and joined using four screws.

31. Two screws through the wide edge of the vertical piece into the side of the armrest, and two screws through wide edge of the armrest into the vertical of the backrest.

32. Repeat steps 30 & 31 to attach the second armrest. This completes the back and armrest of your DIY Chair.

33. Return to the chair frame and legs. Turn the unit onto its side. Place a piece of wood towards the front of the chair parallel with the leg but pointing in the opposite direction.

34. See picture for exact position. This piece of wood forms the vertical support for your armrest. Join the vertical piece of wood to the frame using four screws.

35. Attach a second armrest support to the opposite side of the chair frame using a further four screws.

36. Take the back and armrest section and slide the two vertical pieces of wood through the large gap in the seat slats.

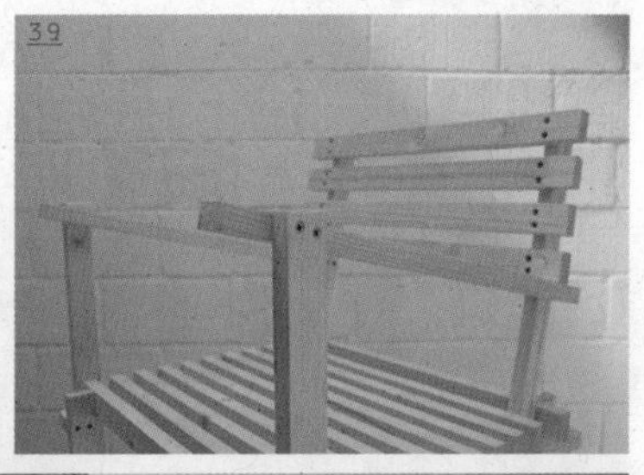

37. Lean the backrest backwards as far as it will go and slide it up or down until the front ends of the armrests are in contact with the vertical armrest supports (see image 39).

38. Using your final eight screws join the two vertical pieces of wood of the backrest to the inside of the chair frame (image 37), and screw the top edge of the armrest supports to the side edge of the armrests.

39. Your DIY Chair is now complete and ready for sitting on.

40. Finally, for the finishing touch, please cut or copy the label and glue it to the underside of your new DIY Chair

Designed by Max Lamb, made by you. Enjoy.

<u>DIY Chair</u>
by Max Lamb
for Apartamento

<u>DIY Chair</u>
by Max Lamb
for Apartamento

Here without you

BY MYLINH TRIEU NGUYEN

I wrote you a letter while we were in Amsterdam. I was sitting beside you at the desk we shared below our lofted bed.

I was thinking of the excitement we both had about coming here, living with each other and spending time in these new places together. I thought about the beds, couches and rooms we'd share and wanted to build something out of them; maybe memories that would act like homes we could both live in 30 years from now.

I looked up and stared at you, but you didn't notice. You felt so far away, sitting there, that the arms length between us, felt like days. How was it possible to be there with you and feel completely alone; that every memory of breathing in unison, sharing winks and passing clouds became awkward silences that distanced us from each other.

I still wonder if you ever got the letter. It said, "No matter what happens between us, I will miss being here with you." It's still true, no matter how far away you felt from me then, and how far away you are from me now, I'll still miss being there, where ever that may be, with you.

PURE' di CECI e GAMBERI

RECIPE BY GIORGIANA RAVIZZA
COOKING BY LEEN HILDE HAESEN

PURÉ INGREDIENTS

1/2 kg chickpeas (fresh)
4 cherry tomatoes
1 shallot
1 garlic clove
laurel leaves
salt/black pepper/extra virgin olive oil
kosher salt
1/2 kg king prawns
lemon peel

SNACK INGREDIENTS

Parmigiano Reggiano
sundried prunes
basil leaves
toothpics

Food is such an integral part of our lives that we realized we couldn't avoid talking about it. To begin with this new topic we decided to ask our friend Giorgiana Ravizza in Milan to suggest one of her recipes. Giorgiana, who runs the Franca Soncini showroom in Milan, is such an incredible host and character and she is quite well known for her dinner parties. Leen, our Food Editor, also asked her to suggest a quick snack to prepare and eat while cooking the puré, as we know you will be wanting something to keep your guests busy while waiting.

Place the chickpeas in a pot filled with cold water and kosher salt and leave to rest for about 8 hours (if you don't have time to wait, you could easily use canned chickpeas, just remember to wash them as well). Once the 8 hours have gone by drain them and wash them under running water. Place the chickpeas in a dry pot with the garlic clove and laurel leaves, and start cooking on low heat. Finally when the chickpeas have soften, remove the laurel and mash them till creamy.

In a separate pan prepare a soffritto with the shallot, and then place the cherry tomatoes with salt and pepper to taste. Once the pan is hot add the chickpeas cream and cook it for 10/15 minutes on low heat. In the meanwhile, cook the king prawns with oil, salt and pepper in a separate pan. Just before turning off the heat sprinkle the lemon peel on top, and finally add the chickpeas puré together with the prawns.

Serve in bowls and be careful because it's hot!

Start with cutting the Parmigiano into small cubes, then slice the prunes, wash and chop the basil leaves. On each Parmigiano cube place a thin prune slice on top, completing it with the chopped basil and the toothpick to hold the three together.

While cooking we also improvised making tiny little slices of bread sprinkled with oil and salt, adding a Parmigiano shaving on top, while Leen also created a snack option if you don't like the Parmigiano, substituting it with a sliced cherry tomato.

AA PUBLICATIONS
AASCHOOL.AC.UK/PUBLICATIONS

A new streamlined website for online purchases of AA Publications has recently been launched, featuring an updated and secure ordering system. Users will now be able to register and have their details stored for future use. The site provides a full listing of AA titles available for purchase and news about recently published and forthcoming titles.

Architectural Association Publications
36 Bedford Square
London WC1B 3ES

T +44 (0)20 7887 4021
F +44 (0)20 7414 0783
aaschool.ac.uk/publications
email: publications@aaschool.ac.uk

BEDFORD PRESS

Bedford Press is a small-scale, fully functioning printing press operating out of a closet at the Architectural Association. The aim of this recent initiative is to integrate the production of printed materials into the AA Print Studio's existing focus on generating content, editing and design. By establishing a direct link between content/design and technology/production Bedford Press proposes a more responsive model of small-scale architectural publishing, nimble enough to encompass the entire chain of production in one fluid activity, from the initial commission through to the final printing, all within the AA's Bedford Square home.

Bedford Press
Architectural Association School of Architecture
T: +44 (0)020 7887 4088
aaprintstudio.net
email: artdirector@aaschool.ac.uk

Image: Detail of workflow diagram extracted from frontispiece in *Cedric Price Works II*, published by AA Publications, 1984

BOUNDARIES AND ETHICS OF DWELLING by ARQUITECTURA-G

conversation with FAR and Ekhi Lopetegi

All photopraphs of The Wall House by FAR
courtesy of Cristobal Palma

Apartamento Magazine speaks about the appropriation of the space by the inhabitant, about the reflection of his/her personality at home. In short, about dwelling and its consequences. In this issue we deal with the fact of dwelling from the whole architectural process; From the project at its drawing board stages, until it is inhabited, passing through it's construction.

The *Wall House* by FAR Frohn & Rojas is really suitable to discuss this topic. It is a magnificient suburban residence in Santiago de Chile. As they say in their website, "*opposed to the general notion that our living environments can be properly described and designed "on plan", this project is a design investigation into how the qualitative aspects of the wall, as a complex membrane, structure our social interactions and climatic relationships to enable specific ecologies to develop. The project breaks down the "traditional" walls of a house into a series of four delaminated layers in between which the different spaces of the house slip.*

FAR (Marc Frohn & Mario Rojas Toledo) are a Cologne, Los Angeles and Santiago de Chile based networked architectural practice. This time is Marc Frohn who joins our via mail discussion along with Ekhi Lopetegi, philosopher and musician.

We present the topic of debate with an extract from a Martin Heiddeger text, "Building, Dwelling, Thninking".

Building Dwelling Thinking

(...)

1. What is it to dwell?

(...)

The latter, building, has the former, dwelling, as its goal. Still, not every building is a dwelling. Bridges and hangars, stadiums and power stations are buildings but not dwellings; railway stations and highways, dams and market halls are built, but they are not dwelling places. Even so, these buildings are in the domain of our dwelling. That domain extends over these buildings and yet is not limited to the dwelling place.(...) Thus dwelling would in any case be the end that presides over all building. Dwelling and building are related as end and means. (...) Yet at the same time by the means-end schema we block our view of the essential relations. For building is not merely a means and a way toward dwelling -to build is in itself already to dwell. Who tells us this? Who gives us a standard at all by which we can take the measure of the nature of dwelling and building?

It is language that tells us about the nature of a thing, provided that we respect language's own nature.

(...)

What, then, does Bauen, building, mean? The Old English and High German word for building, buan, means to dwell. This signifies: to remain, to stay in a place. The real meaning of the verb bauen, namely, to dwell, has been lost to us. (...) Now to be sure the old word buan not only tells us that bauen, to build, is really to dwell; it also gives us a clue as to how we have to think about the dwelling it signifies. (...) That is, bauen, buan. bhu, beo are our word bin in the versions: ich bin, I am, du bist, you are, the imperative form bis, be. What then does ich bin mean? The old word bauen, to which the bin belongs, answers: ich bin, du bist mean: I dwell, you dwell. The way in which you are and I am, the manner in which we humans are on the earth, is Buan, dwelling. To be a human being means to be on the earth as a mortal. it means to dwell. The old word bauen, which says that man is insofar as he dwells, this word barren however also means at the same time to cherish and protect, to preserve and care for, specifically to till the soil, to cultivate the vine. (...) Building in the sense of preserving and nurturing is not making anything. Shipbuilding and temple-building, on the other hand, do in a certain way make their own works. Here building, in contrast with cultivating, is a constructing. Both modes of building-building as cultivating, Latin colere, cultura, and building as the raising up of edifices, aedificare -are comprised within genuine building, that is, dwelling. Building as dwelling, that is, as being on the earth, however, remains for man's everyday experience that which is from the outset "habitual"-we inhabit it, as our language says so beautifully: it is the Gewohnte. For this reason it recedes behind the manifold ways in which dwelling is accomplished, the activities of cultivation and construction.

(...)

But if we listen to what language says in the word bauen we hear three things: 1. Building is really dwelling. 2. Dwelling is the manner in which mortals are on the earth. 3. Building as dwelling unfolds into the buildingthat cultivates growing things and the building that erects buildings.

(...)

But "on the earth" already means "under the sky." Both of these also mean "remaining before the divinities" and include a "belonging to men's being with one another." By a primal oneness the four-earth and sky, divinities and mortals-belong together in one.

(...)

The mortals are the human beings. They are called mortals because they can die. To die means to be capable of death as death. Only man dies, and indeed continually, as long as remains on earth, under the sky, before the divinities. When we speak of mortals, we are already thinking of the other three along with them, but we give no thought to the simple oneness of the four.

This simple oneness of the four we call the fourfold. Mortals are in the fourfold by dwelling. But the basic character of dwelling is to spare, to preserve. Mortals dwell in the way they preserve the fourfold in its essential being, its presencing. Accordingly, the preserving that dwells is fourfold.

(...)

Mortals dwell in that they receive the sky as sky. They leave to the sun and the moon their journey, to the stars their courses, to the seasons their blessing and their inclemency; they do not turn night into day nor day into a harassed unrest.

Mortals dwell in that they await the divinities as divinities. In hope they hold up to the divinities what is unhoped for. They wait for intimations of their coming and do not mistake the signs of their absence. They do not make their gods for themselves and do not worship idols. In the very depth of misfortune they wait for the weal that has been withdrawn.

Mortals dwell in that they initiate their own nature-their being capable of death as death-into the use and practice of this capacity, so that there may be a good death. To initiate mortals into the nature of death in no way means to make death, as empty Nothing, the goal. Nor does it mean to darken dwelling by blindly staring toward the end.

In saving the earth, in receiving the sky, in awaiting the divinities, in initiating mortals, dwelling occurs as the fourfold preservation of the fourfold. To spare and preserve means: to take under our care, to look after the fourfold in its presencing. What we take under our care must be kept safe. But if dwelling preserves the fourfold, where does it keep the fourfold's nature? How do mortals make their dwelling such a preserving? Mortals would never be capable of it if dwelling were merely a staying on earth under the sky, before the divinities, among mortals. Rather, dwelling itself is always a staying with things. Dwelling, as preserving, keeps the fourfold in that with which mortals stay: in things.

(...)

How is this done? In this way, that mortals nurse and nurture the things that grow, and specially construct things that do not grow. Cultivating and construction are building in the narrower sense. Dwelling, insofar as it keeps or secures the fourfold in things, is, as this keeping, a building. With this, we are on our way to the second question.

2. In what way does building belong to dwelling?

(...) We limit ourselves to building in the sense of constructing things and inquire: what is a built thing? A bridge may serve as an example for our reflections.

(...)

It does not just connect banks that are already there. The banks emerge as banks only as the bridge crosses the stream. The bridge designedly causes them to lie across from each other. One side is set off against the other by the bridge. Nor do the banks stretch along the stream as indifferent border strips of the dry land. With the banks, the bridge brings to the stream the one and the other expanse of the landscape lying behind them. It brings stream and bank and land into each other's neighborhood. The bridge gathers the earth as landscape around the stream.

(...)

To be sure, people think of the bridge as primarily and really merely a bridge; after that, and occasionally, it might possibly express much else besides; and as such an expression it would then become a symbol, for instance, it symbol of those things we mentioned before. But the bridge, if it is a true bridge, is never first of all a mere bridge and then afterward a symbol. And just as little is the bridge in the first place exclusively a symbol, in the sense that it expresses something that strictly speaking does not belong to it. (...) The bridge is a thing and only that. Only? As this thing it gathers the fourfold.

(...)

To be sure, the bridge is a thing of its own kind; for it gathers the fourfold in such a way that it allows a site for it. But only something that is itself a location can make space for a site. The location is not already there before the bridge is. Before the bridge stands, there are of course many spots along the stream that can be occupied by something. One of them proves to be a location, and does so because of the bridge.

(...)

Accordingly, spaces receive their being from locations and not from "space."

(...)

When we speak of man and space, it sounds as though man stood on one side, space on the other. Yet space is not something that faces man. It is neither an external object nor an inner experience. It is not that there are men, and over and above them space; for when I say "a man," and in saying this word think of a being who exists in a human manner-that is, who dwells-then by the name "man" I already name the stay within the fourfold among things. Even when we relate ourselves to those things that are not in our immediate reach, we are staying with the things themselves.

(...)

Only if we are capable of dwelling, only then can we build. Our reference to the Black Forest farm in no way means that we should or could go back to building such houses; rather, it illustrates by a dwelling that has been how it was able to build.

(...)

Dwelling, however, is the basic character of Being in keeping with which mortals exist.

(...)

Building and thinking are, each in its own way, inescapable for dwelling. The two, however, are also insufficient for dwelling so long as each busies itself with its own affairs in separation instead of listening to one another.

(...)

The real plight of dwelling does not lie merely in a lack of houses. The real plight of dwelling is indeed older than the world wars with their destruction, older also than the increase of the earth's population and the condition of the industrial workers. The real dwelling plight lies in this, that mortals ever search anew for the nature of dwelling, that they must ever learn to dwell. What if man's homelessness consisted in this, that man still does not even think of the real plight of dwelling as the plight? Yet as soon as man gives thought to his homelessness, it is a misery no longer. Rightly considered and kept well in mind, it is the sole summons that calls mortals into their dwelling.

ARQUITECTURA-G
We have considered *wall house* to be very appropriate to talk about the ethics of dwelling, because as far as we are concerned this house speaks clearly of it and it is open to be analyzed over and above its formal or merely tendentious aspects.

So, the way we see this house is as an example of unity in architecture practice, resolving structure, shape and habitable areas in its construction. That is, we are not talking about a house made by the addition of independent units which are assembled together to give shape to the dwelling, but a habitable framework, and it shows it with no shame at all. There's no limit in-between but every piece can be understood at once. The architectural elements are corrupted turning the structure into a divider filter or shelves, and at the same time every component is bare with its raw materials talking about this ethics.

If people have to learn how to dwell (speaking in a Heideggeresque sense), constructing is in itself dwelling, therefore the way we build is the way we dwell, is the way we are men.

Can a house have a didactic function? Can a house help mankind to be men? Can it link us to the *earth*?

MARC FROHN
I have a rather hard time imagining architecture as a didactic device. If - for example - the Wall House was such, it would - according to Merriam Webster - be "intended and designed to teach". Thus the prime objective of the house would be to convey ONE agenda of inhabitation that could more or less unmistakably be read by the occupant.

Instead I personally find your short description of the Wall House as a "habitable framework" very productive to touch upon some of the key aspects of the project beyond the obvious formal aspects. By definition a framework leaves room to be filled out and I think that exactly this is one of the challenging aspects of the project as to me it marks – both in the process of designing and building as well as in its occupation – an exploration into the environments of living: It allows to renegotiate boundaries both amongst the occupants and in relationship to the surrounding. It is in this sense *unconventional* in the truest sense of the word: By *unconventional* I don't mean "having a surprising form", but instead excluding some of our dearest assumptions of suburban living (that's what the house is) of privacy, personal space and relationship to the environment.

EKHI LOPETEGI
My approach to the problem may seem theoretical but I don't intend to displace the conversation to non-architectural grounds. The way I see it, the core problem here is the relationship between the 'habitable framework' and the 'surrounding' or 'enviroment'. The concept of 'relationship' itself (between framework and enviroment) seems to be the main issue in a way I shall explain. Let me explain this.

When Heidegger reminds us that we have to learn how to dwell , he's never inviting us to search for a certain content we should assimilate the same way we comprehend a mathematical theorem. On the contrary, he's inviting us to deal with things *in a proper way*. Basically, dealing with things is *being related to things in such and such a way*; so we can either relate to things properly or unproperly. Being related to things in a proper way already means dealing with things according with the essence of dwelling. What kind of dealing with things is that of dwelling?

Far from the activity of occupying a certain space dwelling unfolds as cultivating and erecting buildings. Cultivating is *taking care* of things the way they essentially are, *letting them be* what they truly are; that is to say, we don't ask or pretend things to be the way we want them to be, rather we only take care of their growing keeping it save from any danger so that the growing can take place according with its true essence.

On the other hand, building is arranging spaces in the way of producing locations for men and women, and all this according with the essence of dwelling. Those locations make the proper relationship to The Fourfold *take place:* we take earth *as* earth; we take sky *as* sky; we take death *as* death; we take divinities *as* divinities. That is, we take them the way they *already* are, we take them in a way we *let* them be what they are.

Heidegger's exotic argot should not hide the main problem concerning dwelling. For the problem is *ecopolitcal*. From Heidegger's perspective, we could state that a culture anxiously searching for a way to avoid maturity through multiple make up strategies is not taking death *as* death. Builiding up a 'beach' where no beach has ever been naturally produced could easily be taken as *forcing earth to be a certain way* rather than taking earth *as* it actually is. And still, dwelling is not be taken as being according with 'nature' in a superficial way. MF wrote that the Wall-house "*allows to renegotiate boundaries both amongst the occupants and in relationship to the surrounding"*. We could therefore ask wether there's a concious ethico-political approach to architecture in the Wall-house; and if yes, what's the role of the 'bioclimatical' or the 'ecopolitical' in the architectural practices today.

ARQUITECTURA-G
Talking about "*renegotiation of boundaries*" you both mentioned we might say that any house, as dwelling unit, has at least two general levels of limit:

1 The boundary among inner house and the outside
2 The inner boundaries between spaces

In the wall house, and in any suburban/garden house the outer limit gives more chance to think about than in an urban house. We consider that your choice, when

approaching the matter, it's been to blur the edge. The same reading is valid for the (almost non-existent) limits between interior spaces.

When crossing the house from its rigid core up to the surrounding area, we observe that as the spaces have a minor requirement of intimacy the house becomes more permeable up to getting blurred to open to the garden. In order to do it, aside from the materials hardness gradient, the geometry of the layers becomes more complex in a scheme that we could qualify as radial; ((((*concrete cave*) *stacked shelving*) *milky shell*) *soft skin*). The resulting interstices are themselves a *classic* in-and-out space of modern architecture. However, the interstices speak to us of an ethics in the place positioning, as much from the functional point of view as from the formal one, and from the ecopolitical approach that Ekhi mentioned.

We notice that the aim or will of the wall house is not to indoctrinate –in the sense of dictate- how to live, but it is unavoidably a device that moderately determinates how to dwell as it configures a *scenario*. It is the soft thing, the smoothness of the boundaries which speaks to us of a new ethics of how to dwell, in which the negotiation between individuals or inhabitants supposes a greater shock of the one that exists in traditional houses made by cell addition.

MARC FROHN

Absolutely (Ekhi), there is an ethico political approach in architecture of the Wall House as it integrates the environment to become an inseparable part of its inhabitation. Obviously certain aspects of that approach are neither new nor unique to that project.

An important shift in the understanding of buildings in relationship to the environment has taken place over the last 20 or so years: Up until then architectural technology was used to achieve a complete separation of inside and outside. The air conditioning unit (actually called "weather maker" by its inventor Carrier) brought with it an isolationist and homogenizing attitude within architecture that lost any regional specificity and orientation as climate became a technically generated commodity. Since the early 80s this machine-like understanding of architecture has bit by bit been replaced by an understanding of architecture as an organism that mediates between the interior condition and the outside environment. Through that a certain understanding of "climate concept" developed for buildings. But what is important to me in the context of the Wall House is that this project relates to the environment in a way that goes beyond what is generally considered a "climate concept". It formulates a multitude of possible connections that can be drawn between climate, environment, technology/material and inhabitation: Climate or Energy becomes a resource in the architectural vocabulary, a building material of sorts as spatial differentiation is achieved through the careful play with it. What that implies as a result is that the architect gives up his or her position of full control in the process of establishing architectural space as the elements that define it on a daily basis are out of his or her reach: In the Wall House one inhabits climate zones more than spaces in the traditional sense. What the different material layers of the house do then is what I described before as a process of negotiation: the amount of light, heat, the depth of the view inside or out as well as the use of these spaces by the clients, all of those are within the range of this negotiation.

I find it important, that the eco political dimension of architecture does not just lead to an "accelerating arms race" in the material and technological battle for rising energy efficiency. As important as this is, it is too one dimensional. Sometimes it seems as if little thought is put into the question of how a new awareness of climate shapes our ways of relating to or inhabiting environment. To me the Wall House seeks to exactly do that: find possible relationships that go beyond a technological "solution" to the "problem" with our climate.

ARQUITECTURA-G

We do believe that the abuse of air conditioning which Marc was speaking about is already overcome. It exemplifies the context of a badly understood bioclimatic policy or energy efficiency. It is clear that we are at a point where it is possible to obtain a totally efficient architecture without being subordinated to ultracomplex technological systems, popular psychosis or business of the climate change. We can face a project attending to all inputs obtaining an efficient final score, that's why it seems more interesting to emphasize the limits. Some time ago Ekhi told us he considered that nowadays architecture is the architecture of limits.

This is exactly what we are interested in when we focus on the Wall House project. On the one hand, one of the principles of the house is considering the hedges that surround to the plot as the first layer (limit) of the project. In this case, in spite of the covers of the house are getting blurred and becoming lighter radially from interior to exterior, the diamond-like formal aspect of the housing is so powerful and fits so well to what it is (to its construction), we understand that ultimately it turns out to be an object that is closed on itself, without taking in consideration the immediate surrounding. On the other hand, once first membrane is crossed we enter the game of the habitable framework we were speaking about.

At the Perception Restrained MOMA exhibition by Herzog and DeMeuron, Herzog said that the imaginaryof what a house is has an incorruptible strength for them, where a room is a room, a kitchen a kitchen, and a sitting room a sitting room. Just like that, what could be different between the nowadays images and the ones from a Hammershoi picture would be limits. The bridge wich Heidegger talks about is not a static element as far as we are concern, but an element of connection. It actually works as an opening, as a flow. The Wall House works just the same way in its interior.

The other day a friend asked for our opinion about how to reform his flat in the city centre, in Barcelona. We opened up his mind about what a partition means, and that it doesn't have to be a boundary by itself. It is not about emptying or using transparent materials, but it is about configuring autonomous not clearly-defined spaces yet still a sitting room, a bedroom or a kitchen, as Herzog referred to them.

That' s why we are interested in knowing what were you Ekhi saying in that conversation where you talked about today's architecture as the architecture of boundaries and how you see the Wall House in that context. Also we would like to know your opinion, Marc.

EKHI LOPETEGI

So far, two discussion topics can be distinguished from our mailing: one concerning architectural or aesthetical problems inner to the discipline itself (the in/out problem); another one linked to the problem we called ecopolitical that frames the architecture in a wider context. Obviously, both cross over and we can only make such a distinction as far as it is useful to our discussion purposes.

Let's face the first topic. It can be stated that the in/out problem has crossed architectural practices all the way from modernism to contemporary architecture. Although limiting is never to be taken as its only feature, architecture is necessarily based on establishing certain limits out of which 'places' emerge. Taken this way architecture could be understood as the art of shaping places through coordinating certain limits and working on their co-relationships. Nevertheless the practice of co-relating limits seems to be over-determined by a binary relationship between the inside and the outside, dwelling unit and environment, in and out. Although this is not always to be taken as 'a problem to be solved', it seems like architecture has always been concerned with the purpose of overcoming this dialectical opposition. So, it can be said that the Wall house seems to follow the path modernists walked. Some remarks can be done on this, though. The way modernists dealt with the in/out problem can be exemplified with early works such as the Bauhaus building in Dessau (of course, I'm aware of the simplification here): the reconciliation between the inside and the outside is mainly achieved with the curtain wall. A *visual* relationship between the inside and the outside is established. However, a transparent wall is still a wall *containing certain isolated indoor environmental conditions*. I therefore agree with MF when he suggests that there's an isolationist attitude in the machine-image based architecture. No categories as *permeability* or *softness* can be applied to the traditional curtain walled architecture. Climate or Energy based architecture's starting point is completely different. It's not about *transparency* but *energetical permeability* between layers. The radial geometry of the Wall house is based on degree differences between a 'hard' core and a 'soft' surface. Obviously these categories are relative for 'soft' always stands for 'softer than' the way 'hard' does, and this conceptual remark is not a simple trick. Actually, it's an essential feature of the *rather energetical than visual reconciliation of the inside and the outside* searched or negotiated in the Wall house.

One last remark concerning the second topic. I find absolutely necessary being aware "that the ecopolitical dimension of architecture does not just lead to an 'accelerating arms race' in the material and technological battle for rising energy efficiency" as MF writes. For if we meditate enough on the main issue concerning the ecopolitical approach to architecture we'll notice that it's not about solving bioclimatical problems within a *bioclimaticaly blind framework,* but about founding the architectural practice itself on a *bioclimatically aware framework*. That is, changing the whole paradigm depending on wich our approach to architecture is defined. Indeed, this is what Heidegger's text is about: the proper way of dwelling is that in wich our approach to things is proper too. As I already wrote, that would mean dealing with things according with their essence.

MARC FROHN

I think that it is quite productive to bring the discussion back to the issue of boundary as it will actually help us to tie the two strains of the discussion that E characterized together once more: I want to step back for a moment to see how we characterize boundary as I think it will help us relating the two trajectories. To some degree it builds on an issue that A-G brought up, when referring to the "flow" and "opening" of the Wall House. I think that in the context of both describing this house, but also in seeing architecture in general in relationship to a larger eco-political context it becomes crucial to overcome the notion of boundary as object, as fixt element of separation. Instead I would follow Michelle Addington in her argument that "perceptual environments – those that determine what we feel, hear and see – are all thermodynamic in that they are fundamentally about the motion of energy". Thus their boundaries, too, should be thought of in that vain, as they don't interest me as static elements of separation, but more as behaviours and interaction. Thus the boundary becomes a zone of exchange between two environments. From here I think it is a small step only to get to Arquitectura-G's point of the "element of connection". At the same time it constitutes for me one of the aspects of a "bioclimatically aware framework" (Ekhi).

EKHI LOPETEGI
When we first started the discussion I wasn't really aware of how the boundary concept has changed once the bioclimatical issues interfere the formal and geometrical problems. When we talk about the bioclimatical we already talk about the energetical and therefore about the thesmodynamical. The sentence quoted by Marc explains it clearly. The environment is not only a geometrical complex of formal volumes; it deals now with *formally ambiguous substances* such as heat, noise, light and on. Is not that we found new substances to care about determining architectural results; it's more than even old and classical variables such as light or heat will be treaten in a different way once we adopt a 'bioclimatically aware' perspective. This perspective is one in which architectural substances or matters *affect* each other; they're not *contained* in formal geometries but rather they already *correlate* in a diffuse way. Thus, from an energetical framework the 'boundary' is just the *zone* in which the substances meet, interact and affect each other ("zone of exchange"); the 'boundary' between a built unit and its environment will thus be a co-affective one too. The difference between the inside and the outside will therefore be a *degree* difference. The new space is built upon a general principle of *affection* derived from the energetical or thermodynamical viewpoint.

ARQUITECTURA-G
We like the idea of house's fragility, the sensuality of the boundaries that goes beyond the material. A house that on the one hand exposes itself unsteadily, but on the other hand combines welcoming, warm and human inner spaces. As we said before, the house works radially, and it is true that it radiates in a temperature slope. This approach to understanding the boundary is nice and contemporary, owing to the fact that the temperature is (as in Joseph Beuys' work) in a certain way what makes you feel you are at home, and the temperature *is* as a result of the geometry, construction and architecture. This way to understanding the limit, is the way the house *is*.

www.f-a-r.net
www.arquitectura-g.com
www.cristobalpalma.com

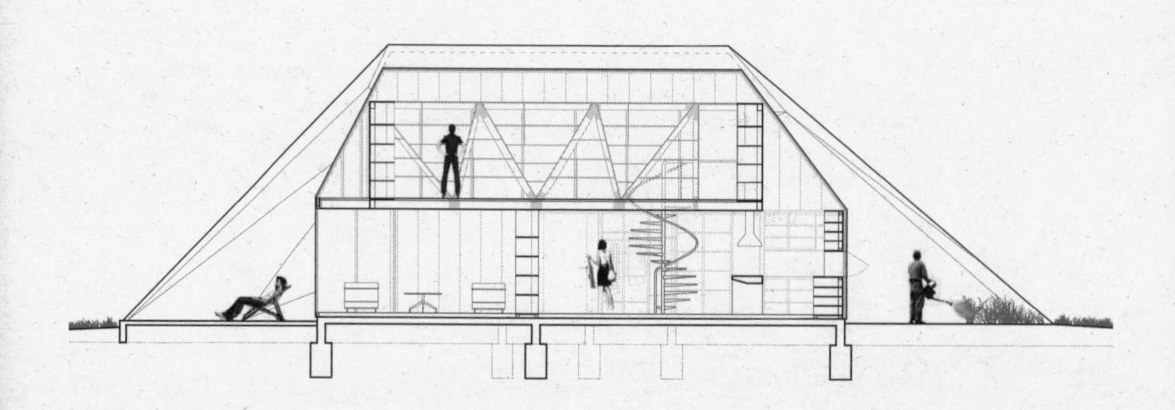

HOME FABRICS

STYLING AND SET UP BY WAI LIN TSE
PHOTOGRAPHY BY NACHO ALEGRE & OMAR SOSA
Assitants: Isa Merino & Ana Dominguez
Special thanks to Maite Maza

ZARA HOME

MARIMEKKO. Aarni, designed by Maja Lovekary @ Eskandal

LIBERTY

SMILEY, *Vintage*

MARIKEKKO, Lepo, designed by Fujiwoto Ishimoto @ Eskandal

Sundtorp

PHOTOGRAPHY BY WAI LIN TSE

Three midsummers ago Lina Zedig, fashion designer for Via Snella and partner Marcus Åhrén invited us to Suntorp, an 17th century farm that has been their family's summer house since the 30's. Lina's grandfather bought the farm and redesigned it to make it suitable for entertaining and socialising. He constructed a bar/disco where the old barn was, a sauna for summer baths and a deck on the river, but left the rest to develop organically with help from the other members of the family. Looking at the all the different wallpapers, objects and fabrics, you can see that he loved colours and bold prints, but also that they have been used in a functional way; the mark of someone who cares for aesthetics but is not really a perfectionist. Yet this collection of charming objects, placed by chance throughout this great house, is what makes the place so truly beautiful and keeps on surprising us around every corner.

NA Bergslagsposten

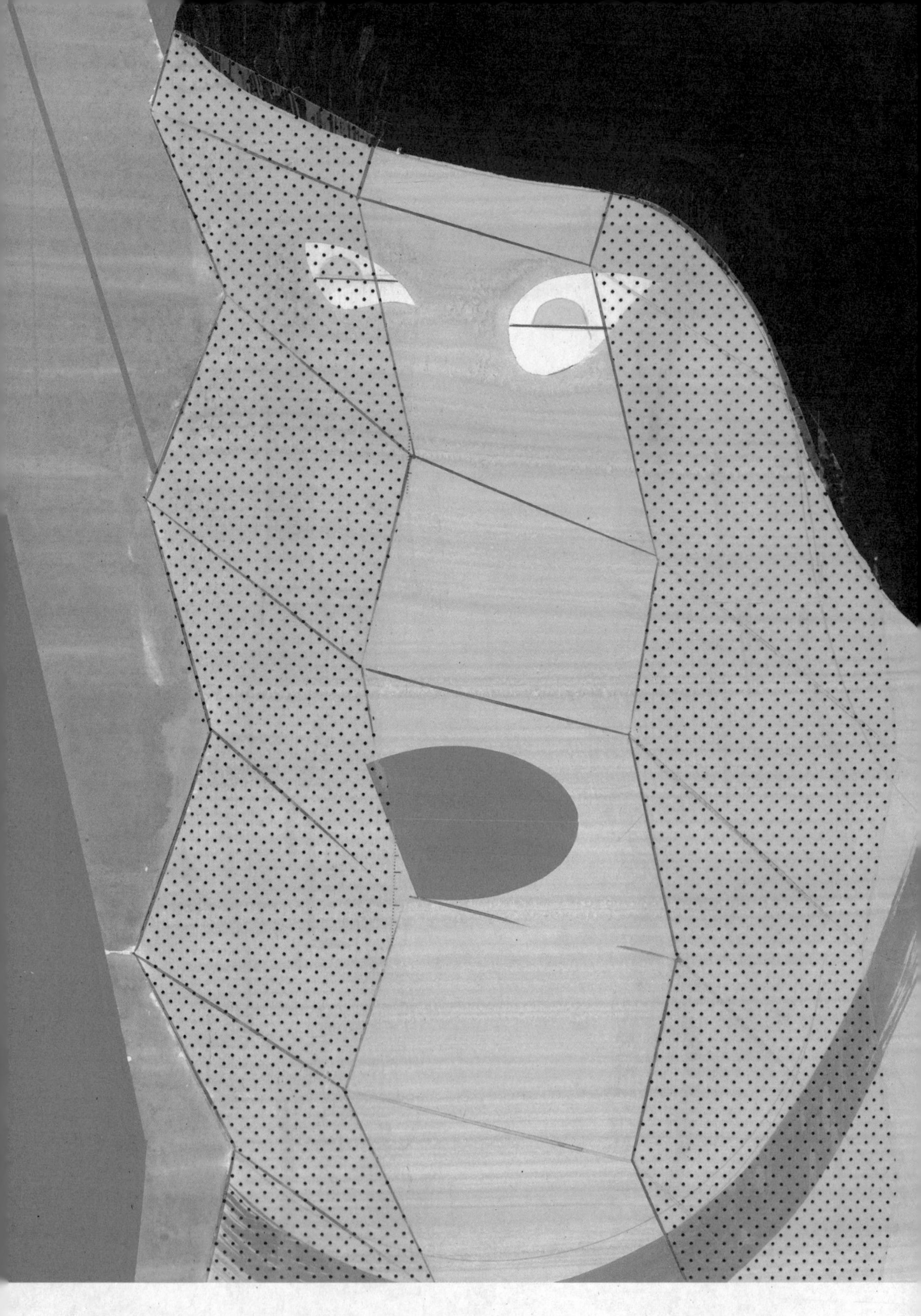

SOME FOOD BOOKS

A SELECTION BY CATHERINE KRUDY

Intrigued by the idea of finding new perspectives and paths into the world of books, we have invited Catherine Krudy, distribution and web manager at Printed Matter in New York, to give her reading suggestions for our second issue. Catherine's fascination for art, food and books brought us an incredible list of publications that use food as a visual source for image making, diaristic or documentary impulses, typological studies and design inspiration.

www.printedmatter.org

John Baldessari
Yours In Food
ISBN 1-56898-495-2

Eric Carle,
Pancakes, Pancakes!
ISBN 978-0-689-82246-9

Ewoudt Boonstra and René Nuijens
Bad Food Gone Worse
ISBN 9070478099

Stephen Shore
Stephen Shore
ISBN 978-0-7148-4662-0

Norman Douglas
Venus in the Kitchen
or Love's Cookery Book
ISBN 1-58234-181-8

Axton Freymann and Joost Elffers
How Are You Peeling?
Foods with Moods
ISBN 0-439-10431-9

Joost Elffers
Play With Your Food
ISBN 1-55670-630-8

Yuko Yamamoto
Paper Foods
www.utrecht.jp

Werner Kriegeskorte
"Arcimboldo"
ISBN 978-3-8228-5993-3

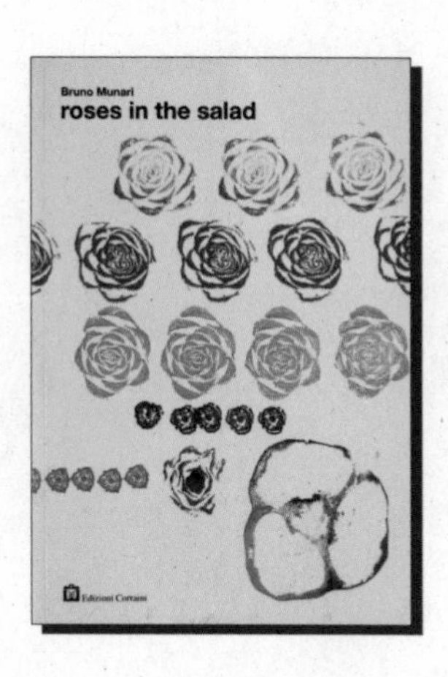

Bruno Munari
Roses In The Salad
ISBN 978-8887942989

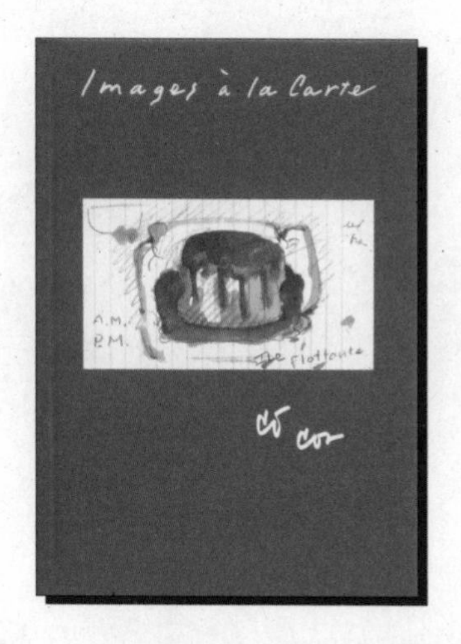

Claes Oldenburg
and Coosje van Bruggen
Images à la Carte
ISBN 0-9608210-9-0

Waverly Root
Food
ISBN 0-671-62795-3

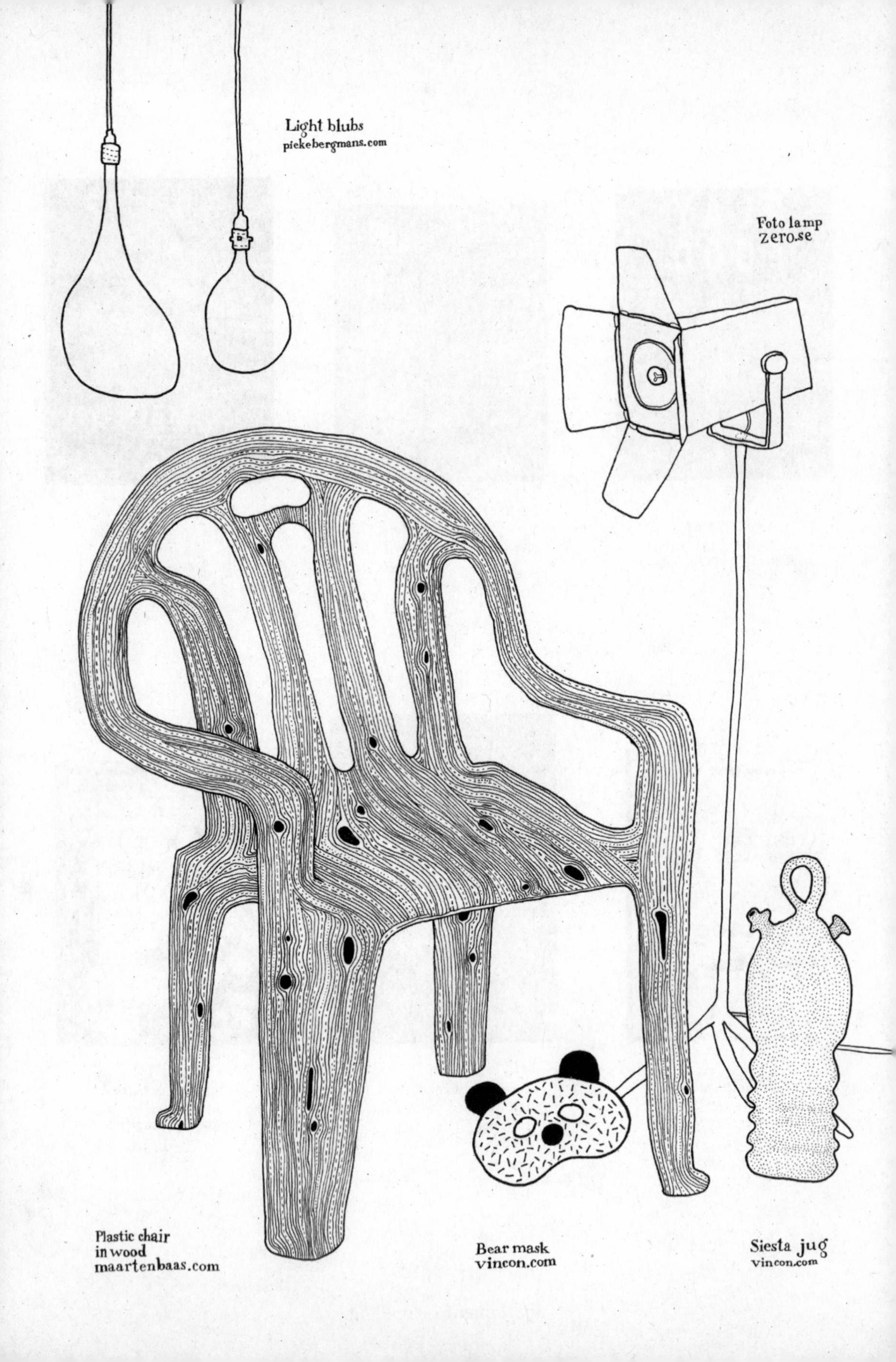
Light blubs
piekebergmans.com
Foto lamp
zero.se
Plastic chair
in wood
maartenbaas.com
Bear mask
vincon.com
Siesta jug
vincon.com

DAY BY DAY

Selection by Betta Marzio & drawings by Klas Ernflo

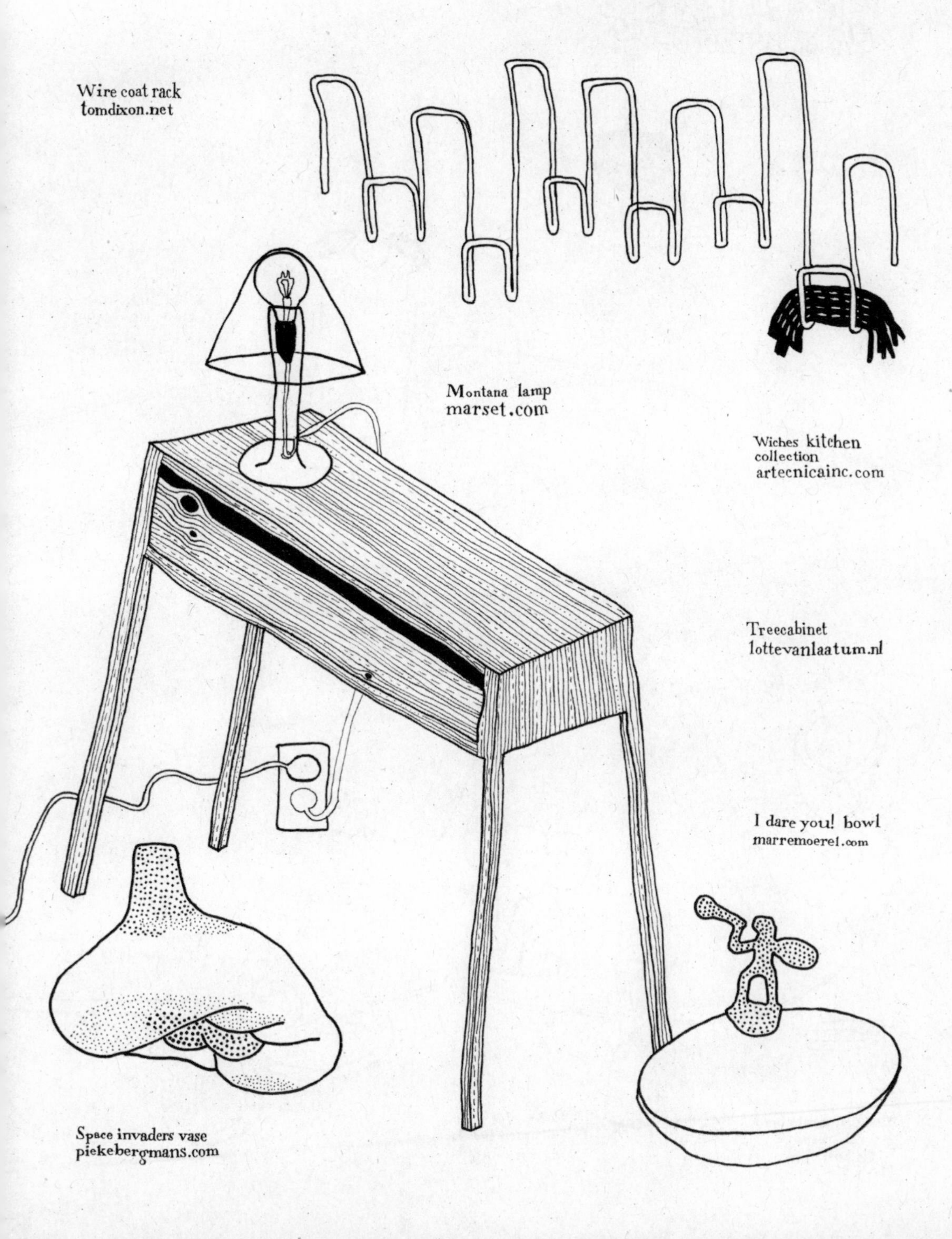

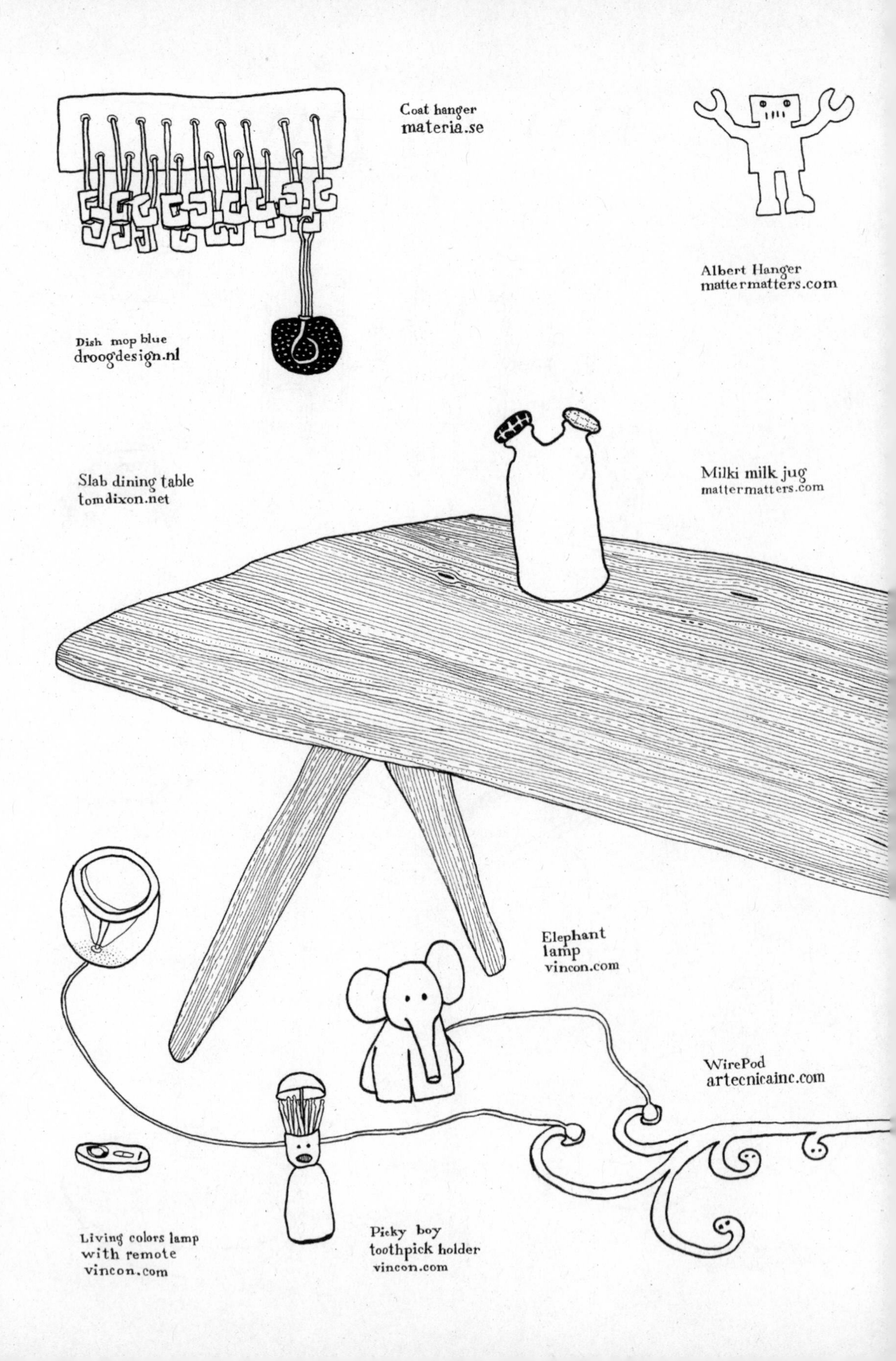
Coat hanger
materia.se
Albert Hanger
mattermatters.com
Dish mop blue
droogdesign.nl
Slab dining table
tomdixon.net
Milki milk jug
mattermatters.com
Elephant
lamp
vincon.com
WirePod
artecnicainc.com
Living colors lamp
with remote
vincon.com
Picky boy
toothpick holder
vincon.com

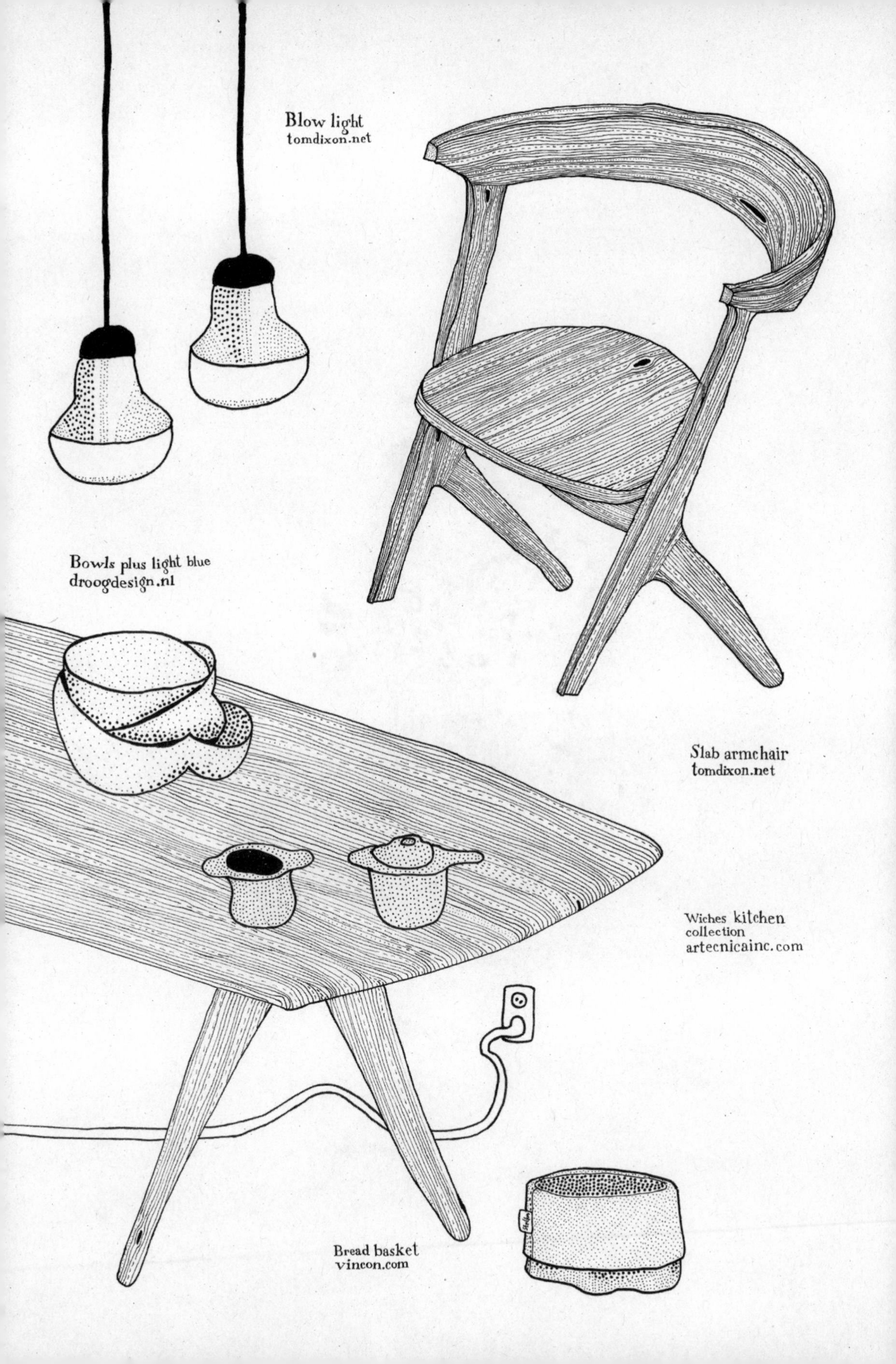

Blow light
tomdixon.net
Bowls plus light blue
droogdesign.nl
Slab armchair
tomdixon.net
Wiches kitchen
collection
artecnicainc.com
Bread basket
vincon.com

TERENCE KOH

the perfect white universe

PHOTOGRAPHY BY NACHO ALEGRE
TEXT BY ALEX GARTENFELD

Terence Koh re-imagines the world wherever he goes, generally in white. The monochrome is perhaps the ultimate trope for Terence, for its various incarnations as interpretable abstract gesture and "dumb" minimalist object.

Terence insists that you do not differentiate between his art, his work, and his Margiela Incognitos; hence Asia Song Society (ASS), the four-story studio in Chinatown he shares with his boyfriend, graphic designer Garrick Gott. Is entirely white (except the black basement "club," featuring the artist's skeletons).

With a candor that belies great effort, Terence says, "I like white cause it makes everything else on it look precious ... black in the basement cause it makes people look more sexy ... big difference between precious and sexy."

This building once hosted Michele Maccarone's gallery, where Christoph Büchel took more than two months to install a maze that tore through the floors, and Mike Bouchet riffed on Walter DeMaria by filling the street level space with a wall to wall, three-foot-deep blend of 50,000 pounds of topsoil and 25,000 pounds of compost.

Typical of their interest in art historical reference, when the Kohs moved in, they maintained the building's footprint, and whitewashed it.

A placard on the white staircase in the foyer reads, "Shoes off fag"–it is preceded by a row of golden high tops. The second floor hosts one studio for Terence and one for Garrick, white with a mirrored coffin and a swastika spraypainted in gold on the shades, furnishing delicate accents. On the top floor, an empty studio/kitchen space showcases Terence's stacked vitrines, and a walk-in closet worthy of Imelda Marcos.

In spite of Terence's detractors, Asia Song Society is blank, but certainly not empty: three assistants populate the space daily, as well as two interns, two cats with minor cataracts, and a young Swedish photographer, often spotted wearing a t-shirt from Terence's first exhibition at Peres Projects, "The Whole Family."

E&G
MODEL SHOP
45
KINGDOM
WATERPROOFING CO.
Scholtes
Sauter
Miele
Amana
AEG
MAYTAG
Whirlpool
SONY
De Dietrich
BOSCH
KUNST
SALES CO. INC.
45
ELECTRICAL
APPLIANCES
電腦改相
帆布噴相
証件快相
專業放大
特大過膠
電腦彩色影印

GERMS,
DIE

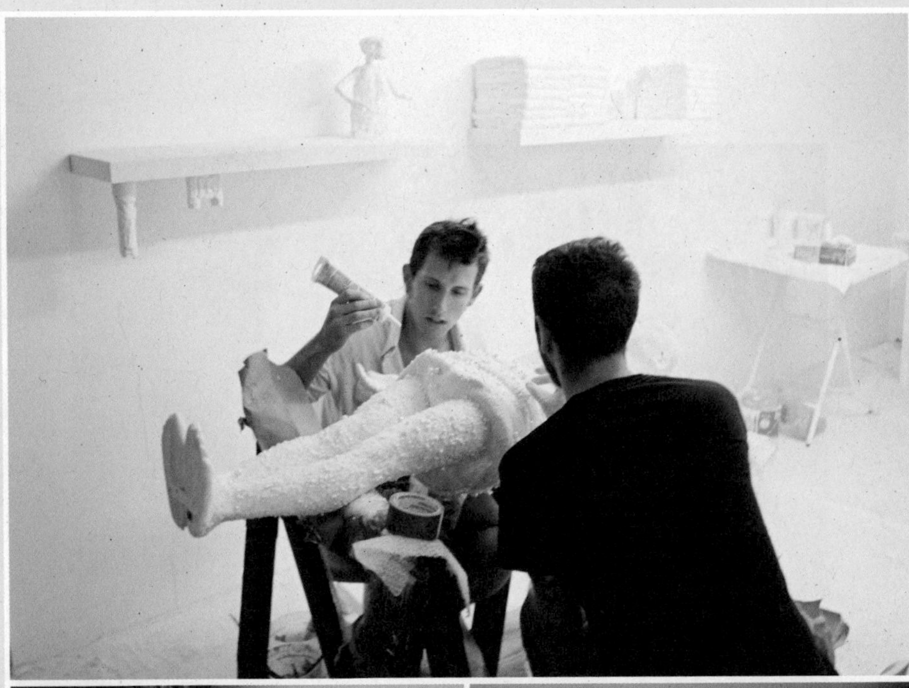

THE NY ART BOOK FAIR
28–30 September 2007
30 Years:
Printed Matter

SHOES
OFF